NATIONAL INSTITUTE FOR SOCIAL WORK TRAINING
SERIES NO. 26

COMMON HUMAN NEEDS

CHARLOTTE TOWLE

COMMON HUMAN NEEDS

CHARLOTTE TOWLE

THIS NEW EDITION PREPARED BY
EILEEN YOUNGHUSBAND, DBE

London
GEORGE ALLEN & UNWIN LTD
RUSKIN HOUSE   MUSEUM STREET

First published in 1945
This edition first published in 1973

This edition © George Allen & Unwin Ltd, 1973
ISBN 0 04 309006 0 Hardback
0 04 309007 9 Paperback

Printed in Great Britain
in 11 point Fournier type
by Cox & Wyman Ltd, London, Fakenham and Reading

PREFACE TO THE BRITISH EDITION, 1973

Common Human Needs is a classic, translated into many languages and read all over the world by social workers, members of the other 'helping' professions and students in training for them. It was written by Charlotte Towle for the United States Bureau of Public Assistance in consultation with the Bureau's staff. Jane Hoey, Director of the Bureau of Public Assistance at that time, and a social worker of great stature both in her own country and internationally, wrote in the foreword to the first edition: '. . . it is essential that public assistance staff have a general understanding of common human needs and behaviour as well as of economic and social factors in the community which affect the individual . . . which would widen and deepen the staff's understanding of individuals and would form the basis for developing skill in administering services which intimately touch people's lives'. Those words were written in 1945 when *Common Human Needs* appeared as a US government publication.

Later it was withdrawn from publication by the Federal Security Agency and from 1952 onwards it has been published in various revisions by the National Association of Social Workers. The foreword to the 1957 edition says that the NASW assumed responsibility for its publication because it presents a valuable exposition of social work concepts, practice and philosophy.

What matters is not detailed agreement about aspects of human behaviour open to more than one interpretation but the profound knowledge, wisdom, compassion and down-to-earth humanity which shine through this book and have led to its being more widely read than probably any other work written for the same general purpose. Yet for readers in another country with different social services and another social security system, these profound insights into human behaviour run the risk of being obscured by references to an unfamiliar agency. It is for this reason that the NASW has given the National Institute for Social Work Training permission to publish an 'anglicized' version in which all the specific references to the US public assistance services and regulations have been made more general, e.g. as 'social services', or 'giving help' rather than determining 'eligibility for public assistance'.

After Charlotte Towle had spent a year in London as consultant to the then new applied social studies course at the London School of Economics, she gave me permission to try my hand at preparing this version. For various reasons it was not possible during her lifetime. I have undertaken it now as a tribute to her memory and in the hope that this edition will continue to spread that truer understanding of common human needs to which she contributed so richly.

EILEEN YOUNGHUSBAND

PREFACE

This book was written twenty years ago. You who open it now may have been a toddler then – exploring, on uncertain legs, the world of tables and chairs and doorways that led to new vistas and corners that contained both mystery and security. Or you may have been beginning at school – exploring, big eyes and ears open, the world of words and numbers that brought new meanings to your astonished mind, and the world of new people who, you found, were like but also different from the people you knew at home. And if you found your childhood explorations bewildering and curious but also interesting and exciting you have come to this day – and to this book – still eager to explore, to know more, particularly to know more about human beings and the mysteries of their everyday lives.

There was never a more telling title than *Common Human Needs*. It says precisely what the book is about, for it tells of the needs, wants, and desires of every one of us, and further, of the behaviour – sometimes foolish, sometimes wise; sometimes rash, sometimes thoughtful – by which human beings try to get those needs and wants met. Because the book was written specifically to help social workers in their transactions with all the hurt, inarticulate, fenced-in people with whom they deal, especially those long-poor or long-sick who are the recipients of public assistance – because of that purpose, the author has taken the next step beyond helping the reader 'to understand': she has pointed to ways by which that understanding may be put to use.

Common Human Needs was written originally for social workers in public agencies, in particular for those who shouldered the tough jobs in mass programmes for alleviating economic need and promoting family and personal well-being. But it was not long before the uncommon common sense that is its mark and its lucid explanations of human behaviour leaped across professional and geographic boundaries. The book was discovered and read and used by social workers in every field, and then by sectors of the nursing, medical, teaching, and other helping professions. It has been translated into eight languages.[1] It has, in short, become a classic.

Make no mistake. The insights and implications in this book are as fresh and true today as they were twenty years ago. There are, it is true, examples that make reference to circumstances that may be unknown to the young social worker, but only these fragments are time-bound. The basic facts of life, the psychological import of such mundane matters as money, three meals a day, going to school, getting sick – all these are in an all but timeless presentation here. The fact is that Charlotte Towle is one of those rare, sage teachers who has always been ahead of her time as well as with it. Foresights are the natural consequence of her insights, and the implications she suggests or that leap to mind from her explorations of human behaviour hold for social work practice today as surely as they did when the book was written. The psychological reactions of both relief-recipient and relief-giver, the relation of policy and procedures to humane practice, the relation between emotion and motivation and between these and rational behaviour, the recognition of the case-worker himself as a person with human needs and feelings – all these and more are set down here with economy and simplicity.

Simplicity is different from simple-mindedness. Simplicity is the unpretentious, forthright, wholeness of exposition that bespeaks complete grasp and integration. It is possible only when a writer understands something so thoroughly that he can extract its very essence and translate it into common human terms. This is what Charlotte Towle has done in this book: her clear thinking results in clear writing. Sometimes we tend, all of us, to equate obscurity with profundity. But there is no such inevitable relationship. Sometimes, too, we hold the obvious to be trivial. Yet what is obvious, what may be seen as ordinary, everyday, may hold in it great meaning both for the human being who experiences it and for him who takes the trouble to look into it. Charlotte Towle takes just such trouble. That is why this is a book not alone for beginners in social work. It bears rereading, even by those who are sophisticated and long experienced in practice. Perhaps one should say 'especially by those'. They are likely to find new meanings in it, new levels of understand-

---

[1] At present, *Common Human Needs* has been published in Arabic, Dutch, German, Greek, Hebrew, Italian, Japanese and Spanish (in a Mexican edition). Permissions now granted with translations pending are Bengali, Egyptian, French, Indonesian, Indonesian-Malay, Korean, Persian, Turkish and Urdu.

ing, just because they can illuminate it with their experience and knowledge.

There is another set of factors that makes *Common Human Needs* most timely. We are embarked on a War on Poverty. The poor, once almost the exclusive concern of social work, have now become the concern of our whole society. Not only public assistance programmes but public educational, vocational, youth and family rehabilitation programmes are being furthered or newly devised. The success of any of these efforts to raise the living standards and the self-realization and aspirations of the economically and culturally poor will depend not only on the money and inventiveness poured into these programmes but, at base, on the understanding – from the direct service worker all the way up the line to the blueprint-maker – of common human needs and the common human ways by which they may be met.

This is why it is of such special importance that the National Association of Social Workers has set out to present this fresh edition of this small but vital book, and why it gives me such pleasure, at once humble and proud, to write its preface.

HELEN HARRIS PERLMAN
Chicago, Illinois

10 February 1965

CONTENTS

INTRODUCTION

This book is based on the conviction that public social services achieve their broad social purpose only when those who administer them understand the significant principles essential to sound individualization in services based on legal right.

The professions charged by society to educate, help, and heal people have become increasingly concerned with contributing to the development of the individual. As we have inched toward the interdependence implicit in a democracy, society's aim progressively has been to afford the individual opportunity for the development of his capacities. This was reflected in education provisions and objectives that were increasingly directed towards enthusing the young not merely to outwit one another, but to live socially useful lives. It has been reflected in medical practice, in trends towards the prevention of disease and the promotion of health. It has been reflected in the expansion of the social services under both public and private auspices. The objectives of social work practice likewise have gone beyond concern with the individual's survival, to concern for his rehabilitation as well as for the provision of opportunities and conditions that would promote his development, thus hopefully decreasing those social ills that in the long run burden the taxpayer and threaten the common good.

The very nature of these statutory departures from traditional relief practices has implied marked change in attitudes on the part of those administering the legislation. Using social, biological and psychological knowledge and insights, administrative bodies have been concerned to institute policies and procedures that conserve human resources through safeguarding opportunities for self-development and through contributing to family and community life. Unfortunately, however, traditional attitudes persist in the present. Specifically, among others, the concept that the individual should *feel* he is entitled to his rights under the law is often contested. Individuals by and large are not expected to educate themselves, heal themselves, conduct their legal affairs without counsel, or get along without benefit of clergy. Those who need financial help together with other social services are still expected by certain segments of the population to help themselves and to feel they are not entitled to help. For the most part, the services for which people seek aid in social security agencies represent a failure in their expectations of themselves and in the community's expectations of them. Consequently the 'give' in this situation is taken with more humiliation, fear of social consequences, resentment, and resistance than ordinarily occurs in other professional services. Therefore, applicants for help and recipients of it ordinarily feel a potentially demoralizing degree of humiliation and obligation. In addition to the able-bodied unemployed there are those who are separated out for special consideration by reason of age or the nature of their handicaps, those who normally would not be in the labour market: children, the blind, the aged, the permanently and totally disabled. Many of these are more largely subjects for protection than for rehabilitation. Since all individuals who are normal in their physical, mental and emotional development are bent on becoming self-supporting, services should assist them to attain this objective whenever possible. When this is not possible or advisable, it is equally important that services be concerned to develop a state of mind and heart that promotes constructive living. An employed mother may, in maintaining her economic independence, fail to meet the needs of her children and thus create future dependents. A humiliated and embittered grandparent may be a disruptive force in family life when instead he might have had the heart to share responsibility and give affection. A bedridden father still may be a force for good or evil in the lives of his children, contingent on the nature of his experience of dependency. We should be committed to a set of values beyond the sole value of economic self-dependence. Depletion of the personality and pauperization of the spirit are evils to be avoided as well as economic pauperization.

Public services are administered by humans for humans. Therefore, among other orientations, some understanding of common human needs and some comprehension of basic principles of human behaviour are essential. The general purpose of this book is three-fold: to convey some limited knowledge of human behaviour, with the focus on normal responses to social and economic stress; to encourage consideration of the significance of some statutory provisions and agency policies in the light of this understanding – not merely what we are doing for people but what we are doing to them is a question that should be uppermost in the minds of persons responsible for administering public services; and, to help supervisors and workers to understand people better, so that they may administer services with reference to right, to need and to obligation. In so far as the worker's understanding of human needs and motivations is deepened, he may learn to evolve ways of helping that strengthen the individual.

Both administrators and caseworkers may be administering a service in which some statutory provisions have been inherited from the past and in which agency policies are coloured by outmoded concepts of what is good for individuals and for society. If the institutions and agencies established to serve mankind are not to lose identity with people, becoming self-perpetuating and rigidly unsuited to human needs, then they must continuously have the breath of human life breathed into them. What is this breath of life? It is a basic understanding of individuals – a growing comprehension of their common needs, the motivation for their behaviour, and the factors and forces that shape men to be primitive or civilized in their strivings.

It is to be hoped also that this discussion will point the need for creative effort to make the most of statutory provisions. Sometimes statutes intended to safeguard the individuals' and community's welfare have been interpreted in such a way as to defeat their purpose. Interpretations have sometimes been unduly restrictive. Understanding of the common needs of the individual and of the decisive importance of individual well-being for the good of society may lead to the formulation of more adequate policies, through leading to critical evaluation of the effect of legal provisions and policies on our services and on the people for whom our help is intended.

If this book gives greater significance to the relationship between public services and the growth of the individual, it may enable the staff to use the agency more constructively. In so far as it contributes to an understanding of basic needs and problems that grow out of human relationships and to an appreciation of the various appropriate ways in which different people meet and deal with the same events and circumstances, it should help the worker to individualize the person and his need for services, even though he cannot go beyond the limits of established policy. A worker with this understanding should be less inclined to impose services and to interfere with the recipient's rights than one who has little comprehension of the meaning of the individual's response or of the significance of what he says when he applies for help.

Furthermore, if this presentation deepens the administrator's understanding of human motives and principles of personality growth, it may contribute to his understanding of the worker's response to work that makes heavy emotional demands. Liking and concern for people that holds amid disadvantageous circumstances in which the individual may respond in baffling ways, ways different from the worker's conception of how he should respond, may represent in a few people an inherent capacity for understanding. By and large, however, a quick and vivid interest in people, together with a liking for them regardless of circumstances or response, derives in part from and can be greatly increased by understanding that is based on knowledge. The purpose of this book is to contribute in some small measure to that understanding.

CHARLOTTE TOWLE

PART ONE

THE SIGNIFICANCE OF SOCIAL SERVICES
FOR THE INDIVIDUAL AND SOCIETY

THE PLACE OF SOCIAL SERVICES
IN A DEMOCRACY

Social legislation is an expression of a democracy's responsibility
for human welfare. Such laws provide a way for us to work with
individuals in meeting their needs. Those of us in the administration
of such legislation are engaged in work of decisive importance. Day
by day ours is the opportunity to carry forward and to make real the
aims of democracy. In so far as we comprehend this we will value
our efforts in terms of long-run gains and perhaps be less discouraged by the frustrations of the present. In so far as we glimpse
the significance of the service in which each of us plays a part, we
may approach our work more thoughtfully, more imaginatively,
and with a more stirring conviction. Man has failed to solve problems in social relationships that seemingly, in the light of his
ingenuity, should not have defeated him. What have been some of the
obstacles that have prevented him from attaining ends now essential
for his survival? What part may social services play in his preparation for the solution of social problems? From the answers to these
considerations derive the ultimate meaning and value of our work.

We live in a period of scientific enlightenment and of great
technical achievement which, if intelligently used, could render the
life of all people more satisfactory than ever before. However, we
experience worldwide economic depressions, inflation, lack of
resources and widespread want and fear which curtail man's
freedom. In our day, as repeatedly throughout history, this basic
want and fear have engendered hostile feelings that, in turn, have
pitted man against man and prompted him to use his scientific
enlightenment in wholesale destruction of life and property that
threatens not only the realization of his social goals but also his
very survival. One encounters here a curious manifestation of human
behaviour. Through intellectual achievement man attains the heights
from which he can glimpse that better life for all people for which
he has been striving throughout the ages, only to fail to solve the

problems that would entrench his gains and only to be impelled to use those attainments against himself and his kind.

The explanation given by Franz Alexander is that man fails to solve the basic economic problems the solution of which would eliminate inevitable want and the most elemental fears from which stem some of his most hostile aggressions, not because these problems are beyond his intellectual scope – i.e. his mental ingenuity – but because economic strivings have deep emotional determinants that involve human relationships in complex ways. Alexander maintains that human relationships are primarily governed not by reason but by essentially irrational emotional forces, and that man's mastery of nature has proved a curse rather than a blessing in the hands of men ignorant of their own personalities and of human relationships. His conclusion is that the gap between the natural and the social sciences must be bridged:

> 'The critical, empirical attitude of the natural sciences must now be extended to the study of personality and to the social sciences in order to achieve the same mastery of individual and social behaviour which we have acquired over the forces of inanimate nature.'[1]

The study of personality and the social sciences is certainly an essential step in acquiring mastery of individual and social behaviour. Unlike the situation in the natural sciences, however, this mastery may not be attained through study alone. In fact, even the 'critical, empirical attitude' essential to productive study can be attained only in so far as the individual's total personality growth makes it possible for him (a) to look at human behaviour objectively, (b) to accept emotionally the insight gained, and (c) to utilize this understanding in the modification of his behaviour from self-centred aims to social concerns. What are the factors and forces in life that may enable man to develop capacity for self-understanding and for using that understanding in attaining more constructive human relationships and helping others to do likewise? What are the essential elements in the individual's life experience that may make him more susceptible to social aims – i.e. less hostile, less anxious, and thereby less self-aggrandizing or less submissive? The decisive point here is that knowledge of personality may not enable him to

---

[1] Franz Alexander, MD, *Our Age of Unreason: A Study of the Irrational Forces in Social Life*, 1st edn, Philadelphia: J. B. Lippincott Co., 1942, p. 22.

behave more rationally if his experiences have been such as to create excessive or distorted needs that operate as a more powerful compelling force than the dictates of reason. We want for ourselves and for others the kind of experience that will promote personality growth and thus a greater capacity for rational behaviour. We desire this so that we may permit ourselves to solve the problem of widespread want and so that we may become less fearful, less hostile and freer to grant to others the freedoms that we want for ourselves. Social workers need to know something of common human needs, something of the motivations of human behaviour, something of the factors and forces that shape personality and are significant in man's development.

Essential elements governing human development
Consider, first, in a general way and not necessarily in the order of their importance, some of the essential elements in the individual's life that may make him less hostile, less anxious, and more inclined towards social goals. Obviously, the conditions conducive to maximum physical health are important from the standpoint of creating a citizenry physically powerful and efficient in contributing to the nation's wealth in time of peace and to its safety in time of war. We are interested also in physical health from the standpoint of personality development. The relationship between the nutrition of infants and their emotional growth is well established. The infant gets a sense of well-being that is equivalent to a sense of being loved in so far as he is comfortable, which includes being well fed. In a satisfactory feeding experience he enters into a positive relationship with the mother, and first relationships are believed to be strong determinants of response patterns in subsequent relationships. On the other hand, the malnourished infant is one who experiences a deep affectional starvation. Undernourished infants have been noted to be restless, irritable, hyperactive or, in extreme cases, apathetic, and these symptoms begin at once to influence their total experience in relationships. For example, the hungry child feels deprived, uncomfortable, and becomes restless and irritable, crying and whining until the mother, provoked beyond human endurance, scolds, slaps or in some way shows her irritation, thus reinforcing the infant's feeling of being unloved. Gradually, however, there may be secondary gains for him in the extra attention given in response to his wails, and so he finds this behaviour useful. We may find, unless the cause is removed and the mother's response to the

persistent symptoms is quickly modified, a child who relates himself to life in an aggressive, demanding, protesting way. He may
grow into a person who, throughout life, will be doomed to
frustration because, though he may get the attention he urgently
and annoyingly demands, the love he is seeking is withheld. For
him who still seeks the mother's love in every relationship, the gift
without the giver is peculiarly bare.

Physical welfare and personality development
It may seem a far cry from the malnourished infant of today to the
dictator or asocial citizen of tomorrow. To child welfare workers
and all those versed in the basic essentials of child development,
however, there seems to be a logical cause-and-effect relationship.
Likewise, illness and physical handicap may become decisive factors
in the formation of personality. In delinquent children we may find
physical inadequacy, a physical defect, as part of the basis for the
child's feeling of bitterness, hatred toward others, and his impulse
to compensate and retaliate through antisocial actions. Just as the
passing mood of any one of us may be created by a state of hunger,
physical fatigue, or the condition of our general health, so persistent
hunger, fatigue and bodily suffering may shape the personality
to their own ends. It has been said, 'Man cannot reason with his ills
for they know more than he does.'

The significance of this relationship for social services is obvious.
The long-standing plea that social security payments and other
resources should be adequate to ensure physical and mental health
is valid. Nationwide services of many kinds are indicated. Prenatal
care, infant welfare services, medical and health care are needed
continuously, not only for man's physical welfare but also for his
psychological well-being. On the preventive side there is need also
for better housing, stable and enduring provisions for employment,
and minimum economic security. Tomorrow's world is thus
contingent on today's provisions to conserve human resources.

Emotional growth and the development of intellectual capacity
Another essential element in enabling the individual to grow
towards greater freedom from irrational emotional forces is the
opportunity for the maximum development of his intellectual
capacities. In the United States the taxpayer takes it for granted that
the opportunity for an education is every man's inalienable right.
In an achievement-worshipping culture, learning has been respected

as a means by which the great majority are unquestionably entitled to rise from poverty and ignorance to wealth and eminence. Theoretically, then, the American has met with less frustration in developing his mental abilities than have people of many other nations. State-provided school facilities from kindergarten to university have been there for his use. This is a great social resource for the development of human personality for constructive ends, and one we should safeguard with resources that assure the maximum productive use of our educational systems. This requires provisions within the systems to make possible the kinds of training and education appropriate to the individual and the kinds of educational method most suitable to the development of citizens for a democracy. It also implies provisions in the community that make it possible for every individual to obtain, under conditions conducive to productive learning, the education essential for the full realization of his powers. This objective involves such measures as adequate enforcement of child-labour laws and removal of restrictions against minority groups. It involves also at least a minimum of economic security.

It is not consistent with this American tradition that the economic status of the parents, rather than the intelligence of the child, should set a ceiling on his educational opportunities. It may be argued that this limitation need not occur. Economic factors, however, do operate both against actual attendance at school and against the productive use of the educational opportunity during attendance. That the child who is ill fed, ill housed, ill clothed and physically below par may not be in a receptive mental state, is an idea to which the American public warms slowly. Perhaps it is in the American tradition to believe that poverty and hardship not only need not be deterrents to progress but also may well stimulate endeavour. Perhaps it is in this tradition to give freely and without fear only that which seems to contribute directly to man's capacity for achievement. We give hesitantly and grudgingly – i.e. fearfully – the nurturing services that would seem to foster dependence. *We fail to comprehend the interrelatedness of man's need and the fact that frequently basic dependency needs must be met first in order that he may utilize opportunities for independence.* Accordingly, funds are made available for school lunches and school clinics less willingly than for school books. The cold, hungry, ragged schoolboy who wins scholarships and rises to fame is an American symbol, cherished by many a rugged individualist. Every social worker knows, however, that for every eminent American cited as a case in point there are innumerable unknown persons who might have made good use of educational opportunities under more advantageous circumstances. They know, too, that many of these same individuals are now a charge against public funds, in mental hospitals, and in correctional or penal institutions.

Officials have frequently not realized the many implications for both the individual and society when educational opportunities are not commensurate with an individual's abilities. First, there is the loss to society of the richer contribution he might have made; second, the loss to the individual of a more satisfying and productive life work; third, the deep frustration that may be experienced when aspirations cannot be attained, a defeat that may lead to embittered rage or discouraged inertia. Thwarted mental powers seek destructive outlets. Deep personality disturbance and regressive behaviour trends of many sorts may be introduced when the mind is obstructed in attaining its full growth. As staffs gain more conviction about the importance of educational opportunity in the development of the total personality, they will lend every effort to safeguard it, through using resources to the utmost in seeing that children have every possible provision to enable them not only to continue in school but also to make productive use of schooling. This endeavour implies adequate assistance so that children may go to school well fed and decently clad. It also implies prompt use of health and nutrition services and of scholarship opportunities. For some adolescents it may imply also wise counselling of them and their families on part-time work in relation to educational goals. Interpretation to the family of the purpose of child-labour laws and the possible consequences of violation may be indicated.

Relationship with others is important for personality development
It is essential that we should understand man's emotional nature as well as his physical and intellectual needs. This leads to recognition of a third important element in a life experience conducive to personality growth – the kind of relationships an individual experiences in the early years within the family and throughout his life in other groups. The early family relationships are generally conceded to be of primary importance, since they determine the basic personality patterns and influence in considerable measure the nature of his subsequent relationships. In the human personality there is a natural and inevitable impulse towards growth from the

original state of dependence to a state of greater self-sufficiency and independence. It is generally agreed that the human personality grows, develops, and matures through relationships with others, and that there is an innate tendency to gravitate into relationships with others in the interests of survival. Man's social needs, i.e. what he seeks in relationships throughout life, will vary with age, changing circumstances, and prior relationship experiences. What he seeks at different ages and how his personality is affected by these experiences will be considered in some detail in the following chapters. At this point it is important to note the interrelatedness of the various elements – physical, mental, and emotional – in the total life experience. In the last analysis we note the vital, perhaps even primary, importance of experience in human relationships.

For instance, a chronically sick child may elicit a response from his parents quite different from that proffered to his brothers and sisters. Thus, in the same family he has a different environment and he may emerge from the home with attitudes and needs that continue to make a vastly different life experience for him in the long run. A mentally dull child born into a family where intellectual ability is highly valued may find his mental condition a much greater hardship throughout life than a similarly endowed child who grows up in a family where his limitations matter very little. Conversely, relationships may create conditions and circumstances that are decisive in the individual's development. A child who is reared in a home where there is marked marital friction and continual tension centring on him may grow up with deep emotional conflicts that are expressed in physical symptoms. These symptoms in turn create for him problems of physical disability, so that his further development is shaped by the physical condition as well as by the primary difficulty, the emotional conflict. Or an emotionally disturbed child from such a family may have reacted with inability to function mentally so that his intelligence, although adequate, is negated; being unresponsive to education he goes forth into the world ill prepared and his further development is influenced by his lack of education, his confused thinking, and his general inability to use his mental capacity.

The spiritual needs of the individual must be recognized
Literally, man does not live by bread alone. Demoralization and disintegration of the individual are prevented, in part, through opportunities to work and to take one's place in the community.

But spiritual needs of the individual must also be recognized, understood and respected. They must be seen as distinct needs and they must also be seen in relation to other human needs. This entails provisions that safeguard religious observances, and, in human conduct problems, respect for the individual's religious convictions. Through the influence of religion the purpose of human life is better understood and a sense of ethical values achieved. With that understanding comes keener appreciation of the individual's relationship to his fellow man, his community and his nation. The need for religious influences is especially acute in childhood and through adolescence, when the individual is likely to require definite guidance and supportive judgements to help him towards becoming an emotionally mature adult.

Essentials of administration

Conditions and circumstances dictate the actions of men. A decisive point here is that it is not merely the nature of these conditions and circumstances in themselves that affect action but also the emotional significance the conditions and circumstances have for the person. Poverty, unemployment, mental ineptitude, illness and physical handicaps will have varying meanings for different individuals, depending not only on the nature of the problem but also on the person's age, prior life experience and personality development, and the timing of the problem in relation to other events in his life.[1] In social services we are therefore concerned not merely with administering services that alleviate adverse circumstances in the individual's situation; we are also concerned to render those services in such a way as to contribute to the individual's social development. This aim implies several considerations, notably:

  1. Since the human personality grows largely through relationships with others, and since family relationships are of primary importance in the individual's growth, social services should safeguard the strengths of family life.

  2. Since we deal with people in time of trouble, when they are 'in the midst of emotions that come from the major catastrophes in life', it is important that we should help them, as they talk to us, to express their emotions and that we should try to understand the meaning their problems have for them with a twofold purpose:

---

[1] It is for this reason that the contents of chapters 3 and 4, in which common human needs at various stages in the normal development of the individual are discussed, are especially significant.

(i) As they give expression to their feelings they may be relieved of pressures and tensions that have made the problem deeply disturbing. Thus, as they experience some change in feeling, they may be enabled better to bear the problem and cope with it more resourcefully and realistically.

(ii) Through understanding the person's feeling we, as representatives of an agency, may through thus sharing his problem afford each individual a relationship that strengthens him. We may thus help him to find or maintain a sense of adequacy in a difficult life period.

This does not mean that all workers necessarily enter a situation with the primary purpose of helping people with emotional difficulties. It does mean, however, that when people express discomfort relating to the problem that brings them to the agency, workers should understand how to ease this discomfort.[1]

The evaluation of strengths and weaknesses
It is essential that workers should be helped to know how to evaluate strengths and weaknesses in family life. They must learn to keep uppermost in mind such questions as: What is this service doing to promote constructive relationships for the individuals within a given family? What is this or that agency policy or legal provision doing to strengthen or endanger family life? It is essential also – and the two are interrelated – that workers should be helped to understand the emotional significance of the individual's social problem to him, as indicated in his reactions to it, and that they should know how to utilize this understanding in rendering the agency's service, even though that service may be a limited one.

The importance of social reform measures
Administrators must also help workers to realize that efforts to meet human needs individual by individual cannot be the whole answer to the problem of social welfare. Within a well-ordered social and economic system there is a need for social security and other social services through which the interests of the child and his family are safeguarded in the special vicissitudes of life that will occur in spite of all preventive measures. The social work profession has the

[1] For further discussion related to this point, see chapter 2, pp. 31–56. The application of this concept is noted in the case of Miss S, pp. 92–93.

broad purpose of trying to make it possible for every individual
to have the most productive life of which he is capable. In achieving
this purpose it works within a framework of institutions in two
ways: efforts that aim to reshape institutions that are failing to fulfil
their function, and creation of special services for groups whose
needs are not met. Traditionally this second activity has been more
peculiarly and especially the province of social work. However, we
are increasingly aware of the importance of social reform measures.
The observations and experience gained through the creation of
special services for individuals in need must, however, constitute a
substantial part of the evidence for reshaping institutions in the
interest of human welfare.

Services should be administered with understanding
In so far as social security measures afford individuals and families
minimum economic security, they have the opportunity not only to
contribute to people's physical and mental welfare but also to make
possible that greater emotional growth essential for their contribution as citizens of a democracy, the interdependent relationships
that impose mutual rights and obligations between the individual
and society. It is generally agreed that economic security tends to
safeguard relationships and to make it possible, by and large, for
them to be more stable, more enduring, and more giving. As man is
given to, he gives to others. As we extend to the individual the
rights to which he is entitled, not only is *what* we give important but
how we give it. Our services must be rendered not only with
reference to the need presented but also with reference to the client
who presents the need. It is only as we relieve want with understanding of the human personality concerned that fear and hostility
can subside. If the full benefit of our provisions is to be realized, we
must administer our services in the light of present-day insights into
human personality. As we look to the future, there are two hopeful
and significant developments: (*a*) an increase in wide social measures,
and (*b*) the rapid advance during the last half-century in the scientific
study of human personality that has resulted in a deeper understanding of human nature. In the extension, modification and
co-ordination of these two developments much is at stake.

2

BASIC MOTIVATIONS AND ADAPTATIONS IN NORMAL HUMAN BEHAVIOUR

All social workers need to know something of the motivations and adaptations in human behaviour. These are many and their interplay complex. A few of them are so basic that some knowledge of them is essential, even if our function is not that of treating behaviour difficulties in and of themselves. These motivations and adaptations serve all individuals throughout life in all kinds of situations. We encounter them in our clients and in our colleagues. We experience them ourselves in our professional as well as our personal lives. Recognition of them in ourselves as well as in others may help us to function more effectively, especially if we can see them as *normal* responses about which we need not be anxious and defensive or condemning.

EMOTIONS INFLUENCE OUR THINKING AND ACTION

First, and highly important, is the realization that behaviour is greatly influenced by the emotions. Emotions not only affect what we do but also exert a strong influence on all our thinking. This is most evident in prejudices and biases, which are examples of emotionally determined thinking. Many of us may not like this idea, for civilized man thinks of himself as superior to primitive man in that reason controls his behaviour. This is one ideal of ourselves towards the realization of which we struggle throughout life and that eventually we may attain in some measure, in so far as we understand the emotional forces that govern us. We cannot exert any consistent control over forces we do not understand. In working with people, then, *we start with the assumption that how this person feels is going to determine in considerable measure what he thinks, how he acts, and what use he makes of an agency's service.*

A mother cannot accept a wise plan

Mrs D, who is receiving financial aid, was advised by the worker that the doctor recommended a 'lean-to' for the father, who is bedridden with tuberculosis. The worker explained the reason and stressed the importance of safeguarding the health of the children. To the worker's surprise and concern, this seemingly intelligent and devoted mother refused to take this precautionary measure. When minor obstacles she raised were disposed of by the worker, she still resisted, and as a last defence against the worker's persuasive efforts was able only to say with much feeling, 'I couldn't put him out of the house that way,' and 'What would the neighbours think?'. Repeated efforts to reason with her on health grounds as well as repeated reassurance of the 'rightness' of this action were futile.

An ensuing staff discussion raised the current controversy as to the right of the recipient of assistance to manage his own affairs in his own way. Can and should the agency resort to coercive measures? In retrospect it is clear that this case might not have reached the impasse that made this difficult decision necessary had the worker understood that Mrs D's feelings were preventing her from utilizing medical advice. If the worker had tried to understand the feelings that occasioned the comment that she could not put her husband out of the house and her anxious query about the reaction of the neighbours, he might have avoided the repetitive persuasive attempts that only defeated his purpose.

Subsequent acquaintance with this family revealed that Mr D had been the head of the house and that Mrs D had always been dependent on him and on the approval and disapproval of others. Some acknowledgement of her feelings and interested inquiry as to the meaning of this experience for her might have revealed the family relationship patterns at an early date and thus shown the importance of Mr D's participation in a medical plan for himself. He was far from dead, as was revealed later when he insisted on seeing the worker and on being included to a greater extent in family planning. Mrs D could not decide on this medical measure because her disturbed emotions obstructed rational action. This decision may well have been frightening in that it demanded more responsibility than she was accustomed to carry in a relationship in which she had played a dependent part. Perhaps it was disturbing also because hostility in the past towards her husband by very reason of her dependence on him and his domination of her made her unable 'to put him out of the house'. If the worker had given her opportunity to express more fully what she felt and if, with the physician's permission, he had included the father in the medical care plan, the question of violation of the recipient's rights might not have arisen.

A father fears operations

Mr C, an incapacitated father of dependent children who is an intelligent person quite capable of understanding the doctor's explanations, was confronted with the frightening reality of a major operation. Reassuring information as to the hopeful outlook for recovery from the operation, together with warning information on the consequences of neglecting the condition, failed to persuade him. Perhaps some early experience was the basis for his fear of being operated on. Or perhaps fear of putting his life into the hands of another, stemming from basic mistrust of others, affected a reasonable choice.

The extent of fears about operations will vary widely from individual to individual. Many persons, like Mr C, are not receptive to the idea that their fears are irrational. In response to the doctor's and the worker's interpretation, Mr C supported his position by citing instances when operations had failed, by recounting cases in which doctors had been wrong in their diagnoses, and he finally wishfully reassured himself that his condition was not so bad after all and that some other measures might be effective. At this point his feelings were fashioning his thinking and his thinking was defending his feelings. Why? Here we come to an important point about our feelings. *They tend to make us do that which is most satisfying, easiest, and apparently most safe. They tend to make us avoid that which is dissatisfying and uncomfortable, that which provokes anxiety or makes us feel unsafe.* Apparently Mr C's fears of an operation were so great that he found it more comfortable to evade the issue than to meet it. From our broader knowledge and greater experience in observing beneficial effects of operations in certain conditions, we see him as unreasonable in that he chose the greater threat to life. He does not see himself as irrational because, in view of his lack of knowledge, adverse experience of operations and fears engendered by the nature of operative procedure, he is actually making, for him, a natural choice. We encounter here an important principle in human behaviour: *No matter how unusual an individual's behaviour may seem to us it has its rational foundation, its logic. His behaviour, like ours, is serving him some useful purpose in the maintenance of a kind of equilibrium, that is, a state of comfort in his life.*

As social workers, we care for people and are concerned that they should make the choices that are to their best interests, choices that safeguard life, ensure health, and create as much economic and emotional security as possible. With all due respect to the individual's right to manage his own affairs, many of us in dealing with Mr C would be eager, even anxious, to give him an opportunity to take over our way of thinking about operations. Obviously, he cannot change his thinking until he changes his feeling. We are confronted then with his fears – they must be eased. Social workers can sometimes allay anxiety, but sometimes they cannot do so. Frequently we are perplexed as to how far to go in trying to understand fears and we need help in recognizing the kinds of fear that may be within our scope. When we encounter prolonged anxieties or acute fears, no matter of what nature, there is frequently the possibility that erroneous ideas, lack of knowledge or adverse prior experience may be their cause. In the case of Mr C, the physician attempted to correct erroneous information and to give new ideas in interpreting the operation and in providing reassuring facts as to the outcome.

Social workers have frequently found it helpful to elicit from the client the information he has about a situation that now threatens him; sometimes they have found it helpful to him when they inquire into his former experience of similar situations. The worker may thus help him to relate as much of his fear as he can bring forth *readily*. In this process several things can happen. The individual has had an opportunity to be relieved of disturbing feelings in the telling, to look at his own ideas and thus perhaps gain some perpective about them, to experience our understanding, and to sense wherein our response differs from his in not being afraid or anxious. He has given us information that should serve as a guide to us in our interpretation. We may *then* attempt to correct misinformation, tell him about other cases, and give new ideas and a valid statement as to the chances he is taking or not taking in deciding on the threatening course of action. *Now* he may be more receptive to this idea, more inclined to identify himself with our point of view about his dilemma, because (*a*) he had an opportunity to express his version and his fears, and (*b*) while we understood his feelings we did not feel the same way. He thus may gain perspective, see his own ideas for what they are worth and, now feeling differently about the problem, may be able to deal with it differently. This reaction is likely to occur when disturbed feelings stem largely from ignorance, misinformation, or prior experience that has not been too shocking.

When the individual's fears stem from highly shocking experiences – e.g. when through an operation the person has lost someone to whom he was very close and has remained emotionally tied – he may not be able to attain a rational attitude about operations without more help than described. Or when the operation activates other fears, the present fear may not be eased through the kind of help depicted here. For example, if as a child a person developed a strong sense of guilt over some sin of omission or commission so that he developed a chronic dread of impending punishment, an anticipatory dread that sooner or later great harm will befall him, then his seeming fear of the operation may be fear of punishment long awaited. When we give such an individual an opportunity to state his fears, probably all he can produce will be vague, general fears. He may even be unable to give any reason why he fears operations. His comments may be of the nature, 'I don't know why – I've always feared them.' Or he may place responsibility for his fears on someone else ('My mother feared them'). At any rate, when the person is not articulate about his fears and is not receptive to new ideas, we can suspect fears of a deeper nature that are beyond our reach. If, after giving expression to his thinking and feeling, he is unable to accept new thinking but instead must strongly defend himself against our interpretations, we can then know that we have done everything within our capacity to help him. We can see also the futility of repeated efforts to cope with the issue itself.

New ideas may produce a change in feeling
In social services we deal with many people at times when they feel they have failed. Feelings of humiliation and fears of the future induce unrealistic attitudes. At such times it may be especially difficult for them to ask for help and to make constructive use of it. Assistance given in the light of an understanding of the individual's feelings about his dilemma may have a decisive effect on his eventual rehabilitation. The following case is of interest in this connection.

Mr B, unemployed, applied for financial assistance. His opening statement of need was accompanied by comments to the effect that he had no idea of the existence of such an agency as this until now. He felt it was disgraceful that he had permitted himself to seek 'charity' and had hardly been able to enter the door when he arrived. Only the thought of his child spurred him on. He felt he must submit to any humiliation in order to save her suffering. He interrupted the worker's initial attempt at explaining the purpose of the agency and of his right to assistance as though he had not heard, to recount how his financial difficulty began, how formerly he could turn to his family for help in time of need just as formerly they could turn to him. The worker replied to this with a remark that in the general economic situation many individuals and families could no longer help one another. Mr B refuted the worker's attempt to ease his discomfort, insisting staunchly that it was not the state of society but his own fault that he could not earn. The worker then directed his inquiry towards why Mr B felt it was his fault. There followed, with much feeling, a self-blaming account of his several recent job failures after a long record of success. In the course of his recital he brought out that his wife had a right to expect him to support her and the child. Before their marriage she had been a business success and she had no comprehension of failure. Since their marriage she had depended completely on him and did not understand what was happening in the world. But neither did he believe that this trouble of his was owing to economic conditions in general. (Subsequent investigation showed that his wife was fully aware of the economic situation, that she was understanding of his situation, and that she too had repeatedly tried to reassure him by attributing his business failure to general economic conditions.)

We have here another example of how a person's emotions can influence his thinking. Because Mr B *feels* he is to blame for his failure and cannot understand and accept it himself, he *thinks* others feel the same way about his problem. We see here that Mr B's feelings about being unemployed and having to ask for help determine what he does in applying. They make him deny that he is asking for help himself. They make him present his child as the person for whom help is requested. Obviously he finds the experience too painful to enter into fully, so unconsciously he justifies his request and pretends to himself and to the world that he is only here because of someone else. Thus he is not yet ready to enter into a relationship with the agency, nor to understand what he hears about the agency, nor is he ready to use the service as a *right*.

We do not fully understand his discomfort or why this experience causes him to blame himself, but it is glaringly clear that he has an inner need to place his failure in himself rather than in the social structure. Why? Assuming that he is tending to do what makes him most at ease, we conclude that this *self-blame* or this assumption of *responsibility* eases his discomfort. If his reaction is purely self-blaming, it would seem that the present catastrophe makes him feel guilty, and we could suspect that the present problem activates old, disturbed and self-accusatory feelings about himself and may be more than a response to the present situation. In this instance, the self-blame would be self-punishment and would ease guilt, perhaps thus relieving him of the fear of worse punishment through further economic reverses. The final economic reverse that could come to him now would be rejection of his application for financial assistance. Therefore, fear of the outcome here may be eased by 'admission of wrong-doing'. If, on the other hand, his reaction is part of a characteristic tendency to assume full responsibility for his own affairs, then perhaps claiming the failure as his own eases anxiety, for he is accustomed to being able to cope with the world. It may be a more threatening idea to him to think that the social order is against him than to think there is something wrong with himself, for he could deal with his own ineptitudes more readily than with a changed world.

Subsequent developments show the meaning of his response.

After placing the problem in himself and expressing considerable feeling about it, Mr B spontaneously brought the conversation back to his application for assistance. There followed a careful review of his financial situation, during which he presented a plan for moving into the rent-free house of a relative. The worker encouraged him in this plan. As the agency's need for certain information was conveyed to Mr B, he anxiously raised questions about the agency's investigations and records. He eagerly set about procuring evidence of eligibility and showed lessened discomfort on hearing of the agency's way of working, the confidential nature of its records, and so on. At one point he asked the worker whether he thought a man could take money and retain his self-respect. Explanations of his right to assistance and of financial help as a temporary boost that anyone might need at some point obviously relieved tension and elicited a comment to the effect that now he was going to be able to face 'this thing. . . . I couldn't see my way out.'

There was initial resistance to having his home visited, since he had not had the courage to tell his wife he was coming to the agency and had hoped to keep knowledge of the agency contact from her. On his return visit to the office, he expressed willingness to have the home visited and great relief because his wife had been so pleased at his coming here. Instead of being angry and humiliated, she had been gratified at 'his courage in applying for help'. Shortly after assistance was given, Mr B moved quickly to look for kinds of employment that formerly he had considered beneath him and managed to get a part-time job. His account at the time of application showed that for some months he had been drifting along, using his savings, and hoping against hope that 'something good would turn up'. Now he became more realistic and, in contrast to his original denial that the economic situation had changed, he was able to say that 'in these times' it would be better to take anything.

It would seem from his response that Mr B's disturbed feelings about his problem were those of the man who, accustomed to managing his own affairs, finds himself suddenly helpless. He still could not give up completely and so he eased his anxiety over his helplessness by insisting that he alone was responsible. He was able to make constructive use of his right to assistance not only because of the way his application was handled, but also because his anxieties stemmed from his strengths and from the reality of his economic dilemma. Had his attitudes been more purely self-condemning because his present failure was bringing to the surface basic feelings of inadequacy, his response to the help given might have been quite different. Financial assistance might have eased some of his anxiety. He might, however, have continued to feel humiliated and inferior and, if so, would not have moved so quickly into resuming the management of his own affairs. He might instead have been more inclined to succumb to dependency and to pay his way through self-blame.

One cannot say conclusively that this or that aspect of a service contributed to the rehabilitation of an individual. A person's experience of an agency is made up of several elements, all of which probably combine to help or obstruct him, and without full knowledge it is not possible to say which are the most important. It might be assumed that the following factors were significant for Mr B.

1. The opportunity to state his problem and to bring out his feeling about it. Note that the worker was helpful here in quickly focusing Mr B's discussion on his feeling about failure when he found Mr B unresponsive to his efforts to ease his discomfort through explaining his right to assistance. There is an important principle here: *We cannot talk people out of their disturbed feelings. They get rid of them through expressing them and then, feeling relieved, they can sometimes listen to and use our reassuring interpretations.*

2. The timing of the second attempt at explanation of the agency's function and ways of working. Note that it comes after Mr B has moved more fully into exploring the possibility of help; the first interpretation of this sort was futile because it was badly timed. He was still justifying himself for being here and so, although physically present, he had not yet emotionally accepted making an application for assistance.

3. The timing of the second attempt at explanation of his right to relief. It comes in direct response to the client's expressions of self-doubt.

4. In this agency the bulk of responsibility for gathering evidence to establish eligibility was placed on the client. The agency's demands and placing activity on Mr B may have eased his discomfort over asking for help. He gives information and effort in order to have the right to be given to. An interdependent relationship with the agency occurs instead of a dependent one. Furthermore, anxiety over helplessness is freqently eased through such activity.

5. The actual financial help doubtless relieved Mr B's profound anxiety over survival. When we feel helpless to survive, we may feel so deeply inadequate that activity formerly pursued in the management of our affairs collapses. With assurance of survival, we may take hold of life again and deal with it realistically. We see the shift with Mr B from needing to distort reality, i.e. from needing to assert that the world situation was not relevant to his problem, to admitting not only that it was but to planning accordingly.

In summary, it is obvious that emotional aspects of human behaviour are important for social workers in a social security agency, even though it is not their function to treat the individual's behaviour difficulties in themselves. We have learned that every social problem normally causes some emotional disturbance, and that these feelings are inevitably brought into the client's use of the agency's service. Whether we are aware of it or not, we are dealing with the client's feelings about his problem in everything we say and do.

If we help him to experience a change in feeling, we may help him to deal with his problems differently and to think and feel differently about himself in relation to his problem. *Also, in the explanations and information we give him, we may impart new ideas that may cause him to feel differently about his problem. Educators know, through experience, that a new intellectual orientation may influence feeling and hence action.* This will occur inevitably, provided:

1. The new ideas do not run counter to deep emotional convictions. Conversely, a new orientation that meets a person's emotional need may be seized on avidly and used to the utmost.

2. There is not a deep emotional need to think in the old ways because the ideas have been satisfying and useful or derive from a relationship in which the individual is still closely tied and on which he depends for gratification or safety.

3. The new orientation does not come from an individual or authority whom the person mistrusts or towards whom he feels hostile or resentful. Conversely, new concepts may be quickly influential when they are imparted in a relationship in which the recipient feels secure because he feels respected and adequate in the eyes of the donor. The nature of the relationship with the person imparting new thinking, or the status of this person in the feelings of the recipient is often a decisive factor.

Interpretations of problems may change attitudes
We have all experienced the influence of new thinking, regardless of whether we have been aware of what happened, to bring about a change in feeling and action either in ourselves or in someone else. When feelings of humiliation or anxiety are allayed through explanations of the agency's function, through information about eligibility requirements or through clarification of the agency's ways of working, this principle may well be in operation. A view of the individual's problems that brings a change in his attitude towards them also illustrate this principle. One could cite many examples from the daily experience of social workers.

In a family receiving financial help, the mother, Mrs K, showed complicated attitudes about her husband's mental illness and confinement in a mental hospital. Periodically she would insist on bringing him home against medical advice. There was a long record of marital disharmony preceding his hospitalization, and finally one day she brought out her fear that she had been to

blame for his mental illness. Explanation by the doctor and t
social worker of the nature of his illness and of the fact that it hi
its origin prior to the marriage helped Mrs K see that the illness,
rather than being caused by marital discord, had merely contributed to it. This conclusion, to which she came spontaneously,
greatly eased her remorse. She became less depressed and more
co-operative about her husband's hospitalization. She could leave
him there for his own good instead of needing to take him
home to ease her own disturbed feelings. That this woman was
immediately receptive to new thinking about mental disorder
was probably owing to the following factors: (a) a lack of any
deep need to blame herself – instead, in fact, an impulse to be rid
of the uncomfortable feeling that she had been responsible; and
(b) confidence in the medical authority of the doctor who imparted the information and trust in the social worker who
understood her need for explanations may have enabled her to
accept the facts as something other than false reassurance.

So, in the interplay of mental and emotional forces, it can be seen
that emotions may facilitate or obstruct the learning process. The
social worker's devotion to the idea that every individual has a right
to be self-determining does not rule out directing people's attention
to the most desirable alternatives. Therefore, some understanding of
emotions as they influence the individual's response to our efforts
may be helpful to us in our work with people.

THE INTERPLAY OF POSITIVE AND NEGATIVE FEELINGS

As we try to understand emotions, we soon realize that both positive
and negative feelings occur in close interplay. It would be much
simpler to understand and help people if they always felt decidedly
in favour of or definitely against a situation, a person, or a course of
action. It is probable that more often they *simultaneously* feel two
ways. Consequently, love and hate, attraction and repulsion, daring
and fear, go hand in hand. As a result of this two-way pull, individuals may shift back and forth in their actions and decisions. Or at
times, when both sets of feelings are equally strong, they may be
indecisive or blocked in action.

Social workers encounter people in time of trouble when their
feelings are strong. Even though a social service is their right, it is
not uncommon for applicants to have ambivalent feelings about

applying for it. Therefore, at the very start of a relationship with a client we frequently sense a conflict in feelings about applying for help. *On the one hand*, the individual may feel relieved, even gratified, that there is an agency to which he can turn in time of need and an understanding worker on whom he can depend for competent guidance. *On the other hand*, he may resent and fear this agency. He may be afraid that his need will not be met or that, if it is met, he will be unduly under an obligation so that he will have to pay the exorbitant price of having the management of his affairs taken out of his hands. He may resent his predicament and feel hostile towards those with whom he must share it. His initial response may be one of dislike for the worker, in whose eyes he feels ashamed because he himself finds his situation humiliating. It is because of these complex feelings commonly experienced by clients that initial reception is not a routine clerical task if it is to be performed helpfully.

At such a time, when a worker fails to understand, feelings of humiliation and anxiety over status may readily be reinforced, thus contributing further to the person's sense of inadequacy. When the applicant feels inadequate, he is prone to become more dependent. Therefore, if we are to strengthen individuals at this decisive moment when commonly even the adequate person may feel somewhat helpless, it is important that the negative feelings about the experience should be dissipated so that the positive ones may emerge. Only as the individual feels secure, has little resentment, and maintains or regains his self-respect will he be able to make constructive use of the service.

Measures to affirm positive feelings
What means have we at our disposal with which to affirm the positive feelings about applying to the agency and to disperse the negative ones? The following measures may be helpful in many instances:

1. Our response to the applicant should be courteous, kind and interested. A well-kept and attractive office in which applicants are received courteously and appointments made and kept promptly, will give the person a sense of adequacy because it obviously matters to someone that he is well received. In contrast, an ill-kept unattractive office in which people wait indefinitely to be seen and are subject to casual, off-hand treatment, may only reinforce his worst feelings about himself. One large municipal clinic was

operating against great odds in dealing with masses of people who were herded together, subjected to long delays, and discourteously treated by weary personnel. Social workers in agencies using this clinic learned that their clients referred to it as 'the cattle pen' and that only under dire need for care could they be prevailed on to go there. What did it do to the clients to feel, *particularly when they were sick and too poor to go elsewhere*, that they had no more worth in the eyes of the world than to be treated in this fashion?

Here we encounter an important observation repeatedly made by experienced social workers: *In time of trouble, when people are emotionally disturbed, they tend to be more sensitive to the reactions of others, and consequently they may assign great meaning to what we say and do in helping them.* We have found that just ordinary kindness and seemingly casual relationships with a client to whom we have given only a bit of service at time of need, may be commented on in glowing terms long afterwards. At such times we have been surprised to learn that what we did meant so much to the person. Likewise, a brusque manner, a hurried and inattentive response, abrupt questions timed to our pressure rather than to the applicant's readiness to answer them, may take on values irrelevant or out of proportion to their intention. In such an instance, the individual may think our response was personal and charge us with having been rejecting, indifferent or suspicious when we were only busy and fatigued. When this occurs, his feelings of distrust and resentment may well be strengthened. In so far as he must have the service, he may not be free to express these negative feelings in a relationship in which he is so insecure. He may, therefore, repress them, and in accepting a service with little feeling of a right to it, he may build up a strong sense of obligation with a resultant sense of inferiority. This, in turn, may lead to a dependent response in which he looks to us to manage his affairs. Placing his affairs in our hands may have a dual gratification: he reassures himself thereby that he is accepted here, and he has an outlet thereby for his resentment. Demanding attitudes may mount as an expression of his continued need for reassurance and of his increasing hostility. Or, some applicants may express their distrust and resentment through remaining singularly unfree to make known their needs and to use their rights to all forms of service available to them.

2. If social workers are convinced that every individual has a rightful claim on society for help in time of need, we will reach out to help the person with an attitude that expresses our confidence in his

application. If, on the other hand, we do not believe this, or are divided within ourselves in our thinking and feeling about the provisions or the rights accorded to the individual and in our attitudes towards those who must seek help, our conduct of his application will probably express distrust. This is an important factor in the problem of *how* we may help the person to express negative feelings about the agency, so that he may make more positive use of it. It is essential for the applicant to feel that in our eyes he is eligible until proved ineligible. Instead, we have sometimes conveyed our feelings that he is ineligible for some particular service until the final shred of evidence has proved beyond the shadow of a doubt that – surprisingly enough – he does have a valid claim for services. This attitude has the limitation of making the applicant feel unworthy. It puts him on the defensive, and in response to our distrust he may become less trustworthy, i.e. he may be driven into deceit out of a resentful need to prove us wrong. It may also discourage active participation on the part of the applicant because, feeling our lack of confidence in him, he may place the burden on us. Our attitude sets the pattern for the continuing relationship in all areas of service. An attitude of trust in the client does not imply relaxation of investigation. Instead it may well elicit a more revealing account of his situation.

When both services and financial assistance are indicated, a constructive or destructive relationship with the agency, arising from our initial attitude of confidence or distrust, may determine his use of those services and how he feels about them. If the worker's whole attitude about the individual's application has been suspicious and distrustful, the interview accordingly has seemed an intrusive and dominating inquiry. This important point merits emphasis and it is, therefore, stated conversely. When an individual has been helped in such a way that he has a genuine feeling of his right to all the services these will appear as a right to which he is entitled and which he is free to accept or refuse. Finally, it must be emphasized that the relationship established at the first interview becomes the core of the continuing relationship, the content and nature of which will be further determined by the wishes of the applicant and the total scope of services undertaken by the agency.

3. If, as administrators, we have a genuine conviction about the applicant's rightful claim on society in time of need, if our feelings about this principle are not divided, we will be inclined to think in terms of his needs and in the long run protect public spending. If,

however, we are in conflict in our thinking about the individual's right to help, we may fear the community's attitude towards our spending and, instead of assuming responsibility for assessment of the applicant's need, we may ease our fears by silently conserving public funds at the client's immediate, and the community's eventual cost. We may then give our services grudgingly, inadequately, short-sightedly. In such instances the negative feeling of the client for the agency may amount to such an extent that his experience of the agency is in the long run destructive for him. It is demoralizing to be the recipient in a relationship in which one feels deprived and hostile.

4. If the particular agency provides for appeals, e.g. to an independent tribunal, then our attitude towards the applicant's rights will also influence the way in which we interpret his right of appeal. This may be presented in such a way as to make him feel that he has no right to make use of this. Or it may be presented so that we convey an evaluation of him as a person with sufficient judgement and trustworthiness to have an opinion that merits consideration. In the latter instance he will be inclined to use this right realistically, whereas in the former he may be driven to use it as an expression of his negative feeling for the agency. Or he may give up and submit in spite of his conviction that he has not had just treatment.

Two-way feelings influence social workers
Finally, we might say that our conviction about the individual's right to services will influence our use of legal provisions. We have learned from experience that adequate legislation is sometimes defeated by limited or restrictive interpretation of its scope and intention or, on the other hand, that inherently poor legislation has been liberally interpreted to provide the basis for constructive services. Moreover, we know that restrictive practices may modify the beneficial effect of our best legislation. Our conviction about the individual's rights will influence our policy-making and our use of existing policies. It is definitely known that some agency staffs either do not make the most of present provisions or use them more restrictively than is necessary. We thereby fail to make full use of the client's capacity for a positive response to the agency's service and to make full use of the agency's responsibility to the community. In grant-giving agencies, explanation of the right to assistance, careful explanation of what evidence the applicant needs to produce in order to establish eligibility, making sure that he

understands the basis for the amount of the grant, clarification of the agency's procedures, information about the right of appeal – all these measures may increase the applicant's positive feeling for the agency in that they contribute to his security. He knows where he stands and is not left anxiously wondering about his status. In so far as assistance payments are incommensurate with need, and in so far as agency investigative procedures must be rigidly imposed, there may be some reinforcement of his original negative feelings about the application. It is important that he should have the opportunity to express such feelings; this opportunity, in fact, constitutes the measure that is sometimes useful in helping the individual to understand any limitations of the service, and thereby results in less frustration for him when all his needs cannot be met. The discharge of negative feelings is not always helpful, however. Obviously, this measure may fail when there is great discrepancy between the extent of need and the adequacy of service. A worker's understanding of the client's needs may lead to a refinement of skill in easing disturbed feelings about the failure to meet those needs adequately, but this skill cannot compensate for inadequate provisions or for unsound policies.

This discussion of the emotions has been presented with the assumption that how a person feels will determine in considerable measure what he thinks, how he acts, and what use he makes of an agency's services. It has only been possible to portray here a few of the ways in which emotions have influenced the client's reaction to his problem and his use of help. It has been possible only to suggest the implications of this principle for workers who also bring their emotions into this joint adventure of helping and being helped. Further discussion of this basic factor in human behaviour will inevitably be interwoven throughout the subsequent pages, for it permeates every facet of life and, therefore, every aspect of work with people.

FAILURE TO ACCEPT RESPONSIBILITY

All people tend at times to ascribe their own thoughts, wishes, feelings and faults to circumstances or to other persons. When thoughts, wishes, feelings or acts are unacceptable to an individual's conscience or produce anxiety as to what other people will think, he commonly places them outside himself because of the inward discomfort they cause. Thus, Mr C attributed his action in coming to the agency to his concern for his child because admitting his own need of help caused him too much discomfort.

Guilt about a retarded child

Likewise, Mrs M emphasized a minor head injury as the cause of her daughter's mental defect and defensively reiterated that there never had been any such abnormality in her family. Much later, when she was secure in her relationship with the worker, she spontaneously expressed a long-standing fear that her own irregular sex life prior to marriage had been a contributing factor. Earlier she had shown two-way feeling about placing the child in an institution − by expressing the wish for placement and asking the worker's advice about resources yet repeatedly retreating from taking any action. She seemed inwardly compelled to keep the child at home and to give her overprotective care. After bringing out her own imagined responsibility for the problem and receiving the worker's explanation that feeble-mindedness occurs in many families without a known cause, and with the worker's help in obtaining medical examinations for herself, she was ready to think and act in terms of what would be best for the child. It is probable that several factors operated in her eventual decision in favour of placement: (a) the relationship with the worker, with whom she felt safe and, therefore, free to bring out fear of action which other people might condemn; (b) the worker's understanding response, in which there was no evidence of shock or condemnation on his part; (c) the information the worker was able to help her obtain about her own medical condition and about feeble-mindedness, which apparently relieved her feeling of blame. Gradually it came about that she did not have to keep the child to ease her own disturbed feeling but, instead, became able to face the child's needs.

Blame is placed outside oneself

In another family receiving a service, Mrs E, also apprehensive lest she be found wanting as an adequate parent, at first placed the total responsibility for her son's delinquent behaviour on bad inheritance from his father and on his associates in the neighbourhood. Only gradually, as the mother realized that the worker's interest in the boy's problem stemmed from a wish to help rather than from an impulse to check on and criticize her, could she begin to admit her long-standing ineptitude in dealing with the boy and her need for help in understanding him and in knowing how to deal with him more effectively.

It must not be assumed that this common tendency to place the cause of a difficulty outside oneself is always a projection of blame or responsibility owing to an uncomfortable conscience. Frequently, difficulties have their origin in circumstances and persons outside the control of the individual. It is for this reason, among others, that we generally accept the person's version of the problem and start working with him on it in terms of the professed facts. His reactions to the help extended may soon let us know whether he is being realistic in placing the problem outside himself.

A worker who could not obtain employment
Mr G, aged forty-three when he reapplied for financial assistance, had a long record of such help. He had been a skilled worker until his particular skill was no longer needed. Then he became self-employed but this too failed and he received financial help for some time. During this period Mr G showed unusual stability and both he and his wife had an ability to manage resourcefully on a meagre income.

When Mr G reapplied for financial assistance on account of unemployment, there were five children, the family was living in rent-free accommodation in return for some service, there were no debts, they had managed to maintain some insurance, and the children were well cared for and were attending school regularly. Mr G had been exerting every effort to get work as a draughtsman, for which he had received further training and experience. He recounted the numerous employment contacts he had made and was deeply discouraged at his failure to get a job in a firm where there was now a growing demand for workers with this skill. He attributed his failure to employers' prejudice against those who had been on a public works project. Careful inquiry revealed that he had become so convinced about this that in his recent applications he had withheld this information, creating in his employment record a gap of a period of years that also operated against him.

At the close of the interview the worker offered to see the employment manager at the aeronautical firm where he had applied, to help him get a job. Mr G eagerly accepted this help. The worker learned that the employer had reservations about Mr

G because his record showed no recent work and a long-standing record of irregular work. A statement regarding Mr G's good record won the employer's interest. Mr G immediately took the job proffered, arranged to get supplementary training in the use of certain instruments, and quickly and happily terminated his contact with the agency.

In this case we encounter a man whose failure to obtain work was attributed to circumstances over which he had no control. The social worker knew that there was some reality for his belief that some employers were prejudiced and that Mr G's inability to 'sell himself' stemmed from disturbed feelings over past defeats. It is possible that there was a considerable tendency on Mr G's part to ascribe his own feelings of inferiority to others and to believe that they thought his qualifications inferior because, through job rejections, he had come to feel that way *to some extent* himself. The decisive points here, however, are that these feelings had some basis in reality, that Mr G did not feel *wholly* inferior in his qualifications, and that, in general, he was a responsible person who was still actively striving to manage his own affairs and was not given *in general* to placing blame and responsibility on others.

While in casework practice we are loath to take over responsibilities a client might carry himself, and while frequently we prefer to help him face his feelings so that he may view his situation more realistically and tackle his own employment problem himself, many of us would consider the worker's immediate supportive helpwise in this instance for the following reasons:

(i) Mr G's emotional disturbance *seems localized in one area of his life situation*, that of getting a job; therefore, suitable employment could be relied on as the quickest and most effective treatment.

(ii) Mr G has shown many strengths and no tendency to become dependent, as evidenced by the persistence of aspiration and self-activity throughout a long period of enforced economic dependency and adverse circumstance. Therefore we can feel free to meet the fragmentary dependency need of the moment without fear of demoralizing him and with the assurance that he will make constructive use of our help. There is an important principle here, of which we can well take note: *When an individual's impulses towards independence are strong and patterns of self-dependence are well entrenched, the resistance to becoming wholly dependent is also strong. It is as difficult to induce dependency in such a person as it is to stimulate self-responsibility in a chronically dependent individual who is almost invariably mentally or physically ill.*

(iii) In so far as the worker had grounds for believing that there was a basis in reality for Mr G's assertion that employers were prejudiced, he might well seize on every such individual instance as an opportunity to overcome these prejudices in the interests of clients in general.

This tendency to place responsibility outside oneself is a common response of people when they first come to an agency. This may be owing to the strangeness of the experience and to lack of acquaintance with the worker. After they have tested out the worker's attitudes and feel safe, this tendency may subside. A sequence frequently is:

(i) The individual, feeling uncomfortable over asking for help, may need to justify his request by attributing his dilemma to factors and forces beyond his control. Sometimes this is a valid statement of fact, but it is not always wholly valid.

(ii) Having established eligibility for a service, he may then spontaneously begin to question his part in the problem and to reach out for help in managing his affairs in a way different from that he has used in the past. Or, in meeting certain demands of reality in the process of establishing the need for a service, he may become aware of this tendency and be more realistic in assuming some responsibility for his difficulties.

In the process the tendency to disclaim responsibility for his problem is frequently not a vital issue. If he is eligible for a service he has a right to it, regardless of personal responsibility for the problem.

The reality demands required in an objective discussion of the facts about need for a given service will reveal any distortions that need clarification. When an applicant justifies his need for a service in ways that have no bearing on his eligibility for it, we have learned to go slowly in taking issue with the facts as he recounts them. We have also learned that it is not helpful to side with him against the persons or circumstances he blames. That is, we do not literally sympathize with him or make remarks that place us in agreement with his comments. If we were to do this, he might feel committed to continue the initial version of his problem because we have accepted it so completely. He might get the sense that we have accepted him because he is completely blameless and might infer that since we share his blame of others we would condemn him if he were to reveal his part in the problem. In a continuing service: this matter of responsibility for the problem may become a vital issue if rehabilitation of the individual is our concern. It is often important that we should not deal with people in such a way as to increase their need to project responsibility if they are to continue to be active in the management of their affairs. Often, when the applicant's impulse to place his difficulties beyond his own control persists despite the efforts of a worker who has given the individual every reason to feel secure, it is owing to a well-established personality difficulty that is beyond the scope of many social workers to modify.

TENDENCY TO RESIST CHANGE

The individual's common tendency to resist change is another behaviour manifestation of significance to social workers. It is a reaction with which we have been familiar all our lives. Sudden change–anxiety–resistance is a sequence that almost inevitably we have experienced and doubtless have observed in others. New customs, new ideas, new demands, new situations that call for different thinking and acting are commonly decried and struggled against. We repeatedly encounter people during catastrophes that bring sudden and sometimes great change in the individual's whole way of life. Some of the anxiety and some of the resistance to our helping efforts may, therefore, stem from the element of change in the person's life and may not mean that he literally does not want or gradually may not be able to use the help he momentarily rejects. He may have to adapt to new conditions slowly and in the process may revolt against the hand that would help him make this change.

This tendency to resist change, this 'inertia', is an energy-saving principle that, although creating problems for people and especially for social workers as they try to help people, has been a useful principle by and large throughout the individual's life. Rooted in our early automatic behaviour, the persistence of this tendency to

live by habit has meant that 'when the best behaviour in a given
situation has been determined by experiment, and through repetition
has become automatic, the mind is no longer required to function
in that type of situation'.[1] The advantage of automatic behaviour is
that it is effortless. Its disadvantage is that it is adapted to definite
situations and is not easily modified when changed conditions require
it. *As the individual masters his environment, as he gains maturity and
independence to function on his own both physically and psychologically,
automatic behaviour plays a less important role and he meets changing
circumstances more readily.* Dependence on others and fear of
new situations go hand in hand. Therefore, the factors and forces
in life that can be marshalled to give the individual basic emotional
security will lead to less dependence on habitual ways of life and
should increase the individual's capacity for greater flexibility in
meeting new situations. In this connection, we have learned that
sometimes a person cannot use his changed life situation in a
responsible, resourceful fashion until certain basic dependency needs
have been met through supportive help of one sort or another.

A dependent widow is discouraged about management

Mrs L, a widow with three dependent children ranging in age from
seven years to six months, sought the worker's help in finding a
place for the children in order that she might go out to work. As
this request was considered with her, she showed marked anxiety
about leaving the children lest they should not receive good care
and also lest her husband's people should condemn her as an
irresponsible and unloving mother. As the possibility of remaining
at home with a plan for continuing financial assistance was
explored with her, she revealed that she was deeply discouraged
over managing the two older boys. Their father had spent so
much time with them and he had been such a help in disciplining
them, that they missed him and had not been the same since his
death. She had had difficulty managing the money – her husband
did the major part of the family purchasing and planning and she
had been lost and confused in trying to make ends meet. She felt
lost even in meal planning, as she always planned around his likes
and dislikes. She had been depressed and lonely and her moods
affected the children. Her husband was a sociable man who liked a
good time. He would pile them all into the car and off they would

[1] Franz Alexander, MD, *Our Age of Unreason; A Study of the Irrational Forces in Social Life*, 1st edn, Philadelphia: J. B. Lippincott Co., 1942, pp. 144–8.

go for picnics or to visit friends he had made at work. Now they had no car and she had lost touch with his friends. On this occasion, the worker proffered the agency's help in budget planning and advising her on child care, and also offered to help her find certain community resources she might find useful in rearing her family on a smaller income than they had formerly had. Mrs L was appreciative of the worker's interest and in the subsequent months made eager and productive use of the supportive help given.

One notes that, prior to this time, the agency's service had been restricted to a money payment. This lack raises many questions. One can appreciate that the worker may have been hesitant at the start about seeming to take over management of this woman's affairs. In connection with unrestricted money payments, it is important that a client should be left free to plan and spend as he wills. In carrying out this principle to the letter of the law, we need not withhold help that the individual either seeks or readily accepts when offered. Perhaps in the long run, there were certain values for this woman in attempting to struggle along on her own. It might be maintained that experiencing a deep need for help following the loss of one on whom she was very dependent would incline her to more eager, productive, and less resentful use of help when it came in response to her expressed need. One wonders, however, whether she might not have been helped earlier to meet the great change that was suddenly imposed on her.

Perhaps this case again emphasizes the need to learn the relationship patterns that have previously existed in a family. Had we known the dependent role played by this mother, we might have proffered casework services earlier. Perhaps she could not have used them. Early observations in the record are to the effect that she seemed vague and unresponsive, and it is possible that she was absorbed in her grief and too confused to participate in planning until she turned to the worker with a decisive issue. Did the vagueness and unresponsiveness mean that she was *then* unable to use help, or did it mean that she was too crushed to articulate her need for it? We know that when deeply hurt, as sometimes when acutely ill, the individual withdraws from asking for the aid he both needs and can use. While there might be a difference in point of view on this in the field of practice, some of us would feel better satisfied had the worker tested out the woman's capacity to use help at an early date. A flexible readiness to be guided by the nature of the client's response would have been the worker's safeguard against forcing services on her. It is clear that we took pains to leave her free to be self-determining, an opportunity she could not use productively until her problem was shared and she was given certain supportive help in taking over a new way of life.

REGRESSION TO EARLIER SATISFACTORY BEHAVIOUR

Closely related to this tendency to resist change is the behaviour adaptation known as regression. As the individual gradually proceeds from the complete dependency of infancy and early childhood, his progress is smooth and uninterrupted by phases of regression *only in so far as the demands of his external world are appropriately timed to his physical and psychological readiness to master his environment. Since throughout the course of life the individual's life experiences seldom are so timed, fragmentary regressions are usual.* If described by a graph, the growth process from infancy to maturity would show a marked movement forward with slight movement backward from time to time. *It is only natural when life becomes markedly difficult that there is a tendency to return to earlier satisfactory life periods.* Each period in which the child makes a good adjustment can serve as a phase to which he may return later in life. If obstacles continue to prevent forward movement, these periods at which his responses are 'frozen' may serve as a point of fixation. Regression, however, *need not be permanent* if the individual can be strengthened to meet the demands of life and/or excessive environmental frustrations can be eased.

This is a decisive point, one that gives significance to much of our work with people. We are all familiar with manifestations of regressive behaviour, although we may not have known them by this name and we may not have been aware of the purpose of this behaviour. For example:

(i) An infant reaches out to take his first steps, and before he has gained any security in this great venture he has a bad fall. Temporarily he retreats to crawling and may even wish to be carried again. As his confidence is restored through the comfort thereby received, he gains courage to set forth again.

(ii) A young child has just begun to experience periods of separation from his mother but still has some anxiety about leaving her. A baby arrives to take the place he is not yet ready to give up or even to share. He seeks a return to his infancy through behaviour that conscripts the mother's concern and attention in symptoms such as bed-wetting, soiling, thumb-sucking, crying, whining and the like.

(iii) An adolescent moves out into his initial relationship with a member of the opposite sex. He experiences defeat and retreats at least temporarily to his own sex, and becomes absorbed again in the interests and activities of a younger group.

(iv) A man struggles against odds to maintain a place as wage earner, head of his family, and strives to meet the demands of his dependent children. He experiences prolonged frustration through unemployment, which brings a feeling of loss of status in the eyes of the world and of unworthiness in the eyes of his wife and children. So he returns to a life period of being the irresponsible boy who goes out with the gang and gets drunk, demands mothering from his wife, and competes with his children for first place in her concern and attention.

(v) The elderly person becomes physically inadequate, unable to continue his work, and no longer needed by his children. He suffers relationship losses through the death of those who mean much to him. The present becomes inordinately painful and the future is threatening, so he is driven to the past as an escape both from the present and the future.[1]

Regression to the past, generally to a state of childish dependence, is forced on the individual by frustrating circumstances and by frustration in the human contacts of life. In the adult, except in outright mental illness, it is never complete, for it is met by the contrary desire to remain adult. In the case of Mr G for example, we saw a fragmentary regression in his inability to handle his affairs alone in the matter of getting a job. We saw Mrs L on the verge of flight from the responsibilities of motherhood at a point when they had become overwhelming. Her actual capacity for self-dependence,

[1] The grossly childish behaviour we know as the state of senility frequently stems from organic brain change in the ageing process. The extent to which frustrating life circumstances are a factor in these cases may be obscured by an organic condition. Childish behaviour may occur, however, entirely in response to frustration.

revealed in her subsequent response to the help given, was greater than might have been expected from the impression given in the interview recorded earlier. On the verge of turning back from adult responsibilities, her desire to remain adult was expressed in her concern for the welfare of the children and in her anticipation of criticism from her husband's people.

We see people in time of trouble when the pressures of life have not necessarily been timed to their readiness to deal with them and, therefore, regressive impulses are at least temporarily in the foreground. Furthermore, there are elements in the setting of the social services that may provoke or reinforce regressive tendencies.

In general, individuals can be helped in relation to this conflict in several ways: (a) through contributing to the individual's chances of survival in a competitive social system in which the responsibilities of adulthood are heightened or at times abruptly taken away; (b) through rendering services that meet dependency needs in such a way as not to undermine the adult impulses; (c) through affording opportunities for growth and through removing obstacles to growth – all services that safeguard or strengthen man's physical, mental and emotional welfare can well reinforce the adult impulses; (d) in the midst of an overwhelming present, the individual may need supportive help in looking to and in planning for the future. When he has an untenable present and no outlook for the future, his only recourse is to the past. Since the adaptive mechanism of regression has different treatment significance at different ages, more specific discussion will be made later of how we may use our understanding of its meaning.

THE INEVITABLE IMPULSE TOWARDS PROGRESSION

There is evidence in human behaviour that, in contrast to the tendency towards resistance to change and regression to the past, there is also a strong and *inevitable impulse towards progression. There is movement into new experience, giving of self to creative activity, giving of energy to work that serves a purpose beyond the objective of mere survival, giving of self in relationships that contribute to and gratify others as well as serve the purpose of self-gratification.* Just as the physical organism when it reaches its limits of growth tends to reproduce itself, so the human personality in the process of maturing begins to reach out beyond itself. Franz Alexander considers the impulse to expand beyond the limits of self to be basic. It is his impression that this occurs when a point of saturation is reached. He comments:

> 'Sexuality proper is the expression of the surplus energy of the mature organism as a whole. As a container filled with water overflows, so the mature organism cannot any longer add to its own completion, and the tendency towards personal growth gives place to reproduction, which is nothing but growth beyond the limits of the individual person. . . .
>
> 'Sexual desire and love, and the desire and care for children are not the only indications of maturity. The creative tendencies of other sorts contributing to the interests of society at large are parallel expressions of this surplus energy. The whole range from totem poles to modern sculpture, music and painting, as well as the discoveries of science, are products of this creative activity. Most economic activities are similarly motivated – though utilitarian factors co-operate – as can be seen in the peasant's attitude towards the soil or the artisan's towards his handicraft, or the industrialist towards his plant.'[1]

He comments further that the creative urge differs from the utilitarian one of automatic behaviour and the regressive tendency in that it is not seeking saving of energy. Instead, it prompts the expenditure of energy that is no longer needed for the selfish purposes of the growing organism that has reached its limit of personal growth. The emphasis in all creative activities goes beyond self-centred aims.

This growth principle has considerable importance for social workers in their efforts to understand and to help people. It means briefly that, in so far as the individual's physical, mental and emotional needs are adequately met during the early years of life, he will move spontaneously in the direction of growth, reaching out from self-centred absorption in an infantile sort of existence to the more social concerns of maturity. It means also that if his needs during childhood have been met in decent measure, he will carry into adult years considerable stamina to resist regression. Obstacles to continued growth will have varying values. They may be frustrating and thereby provoke irritation or rage. The decisive point here is that he will struggle to keep intact his identity as an adult and will find discomfort as well as gratification in his momentary regressive responses. Throughout the years, social workers

[1] Alexander, *op. cit.*, pp. 206–8.

have observed much to prove the validity of this principle. We have seen many individuals who were seemingly demoralized weather a period of prolonged adversity with a surprising resilience and with a capacity to bury the past and move on. *Man normally desires a life beyond the narrow confines of an infantile self. He wants to learn, he wants to marry and to establish a family, he wants to work, he wants a participating and contributing part in the life of the community. He is deeply frustrated when he is denied the requisite opportunities for this fuller life.*

The social work profession deals with people who are experiencing some breakdown in their capacity to cope unaided with their own affairs. This breakdown may be owing primarily to external forces beyond the control of the person, or it may be owing partly, largely or entirely to factors within the person, i.e. he may have created his social dilemma. Whether the social problem is predominantly of external or internal origin, the growth forces that carry the individual beyond absorption in himself to creative activity and to living in constructive relationships with others may well have been obstructed, so that regressive solutions are frequently sought or may have become well entrenched. Experience has shown the individual's resistance to suddenly imposed change as well as his recourse to earlier satisfactory modes of behaviour. In many of our contacts with people in all walks of life we have perceived that lack of 'surplus energy' to give beyond the limits of individual need – a lack engendered by a meagre life that has afforded more deprivation, frustration and hostility than gratification, realization and love, both in relationships and in the force of circumstances. We know all too well that the meagre life guarantees the ascendancy of man's infantile self and that it does not develop individuals mentally and emotionally constituted to carry forward constructively the aims of a democracy.

When we see the relationship between social security and social services provisions, and the growth of the individual, perhaps we are both discouraged and encouraged. Perhaps we are enabled to look beyond some of the discouraging limitations that beset us in our daily struggle to help people. Perhaps we are challenged also to obtain for people more nearly adequate assurance of their right not merely to survive but to live in a fuller sense of the word. The attainment of such a world implies support of sound social and economic measures. Whatever the limitation of our present services, we can take heart in our labours in the realization that we are pioneers in the effort to make real man's claim of right on society.

PART TWO

COMMON HUMAN NEEDS IN RELATION TO
THE PROVISION OF SOCIAL SERVICES

As individuals apply for social services they may reveal both economic needs and many other needs. In a money economy, money means different things to different people, and its import for the individual will determine the meaning for him of his right to social security benefits. More often than not he will feel, in addition to discomfort produced by actual want, some discomfort in applying for and in receiving assistance as distinct from social insurance benefits. Furthermore, the worker's feelings about economic dependency will influence his ways of helping and thereby affect the value of assistance for the client. The individual's needs and their emotional value for him, in relation to services rendered and attitudes encountered, are decisive in determining constructive or destructive use of the experience.

What, then, are the common human needs and feelings to which services should be oriented? In general, we have noted the need to be well fed, properly clothed and adequately housed as a basis for both physical and mental health. We have remarked also the need for educational, recreational and religious opportunities under conditions conducive to the furtherance of physical, mental, and spiritual growth. The need for satisfying human relationships as a basis for physical, mental and spiritual well-being has been mentioned. Since all our needs have varying significance at different ages under differing circumstances, it is essential that we should consider them more specifically. As a general background for social workers, certain universal needs will therefore be presented and their relative importance at different age levels and under varying life conditions commented on. In order that normal development of the individual may be safeguarded as assistance is provided, the following chapters will cover their particular significance in this context.

3

INFANCY, CHILDHOOD AND YOUTH

The most basic impulse in any organism is the impulse to survive. The need to feel secure – i.e. safe as an assurance of survival – is fundamental. *Fear emerges quickly when survival is threatened.* The human being has a long period of physical inability to survive without the care of others. Normally, therefore, at the start of life he is acutely fearful and may become chronically anxious if he cannot depend on others. He is born with certain equipment that is essential for maintaining life, i.e. the sucking reflex and such functions as digestion, absorption, elimination, respiration and circulation. Initially his only inherent sources of security are vested in these bodily processes, and this explains why regular feeding, regular elimination, and good physical health are important for his early feelings of security. This is why the infant readily turns to sucking his thumb as solace when fatigued or discomfited and why a baby who has had respiratory difficulties, gastric disturbances or the like may quickly develop anxieties as expressed in restlessness, 'nervousness', undue fearfulness and so on, after the subsidence of the acute illness.

The infant is equipped also with a capacity to learn, and this capacity has been described as 'a fundamental biological function of every living organism and ... indispensable to life'. On the subject of adaptive behaviour of the infant, Franz Alexander writes:

'It has to learn by practice ... almost all its functions in relation to its environment, for it inherits ready-made only its internal vegetative functions and the suckling reflex. It must learn muscular co-ordination: how to use its hands and feet, how to walk and keep its equilibrium, to focus its eyes, to speak and to establish and maintain associations with other human beings. ...

'The infant is dependent upon the parents, but through learning acquires certain faculties in the exercise of which he can dispense with this dependence.'[1]

[1] Franz Alexander, MD, *Our Age of Unreason; A Study of the Irrational Forces in Social Life*, 1st edn, Philadelphia: J. B. Lippincott Co., 1942, pp. 141–2.

THE INFANT NEEDS LOVE, CARE AND A CHANCE TO LEARN

The infant, then, has three sources of security that enable him to feel safe and, therefore, to experience a satisfying relationship with others: (a) consistent physical care and conditions conducive to good health which are necessary for a feeling of well-being; (b) uninterrupted opportunity to learn and reassuring encouragement to persist in learning through sympathetic attention to his hurts when his first learning efforts endanger his safety; (c) relationships in which he is loved. Since actually the infant cannot survive alone in spite of learning efforts and since he soon gets the sense that his physical well-being is provided by others and will continue to be provided in so far as he is loved, in the last analysis, then, 'the child's security depends wholly *on being loved and cared for* by adults so that the wish to be cared for is *the central issue of his life*'.[1]

Denial of opportunity to learn may cause emotional disturbance
There are many significant implications in these sources of security, notably that the impulse to learn is basic and related to the impulse for survival. *Therefore, learning eases anxiety, and consequently the denial of opportunity to learn or frustration in learning may produce emotional disturbance.* The infant's complete helplessness and the child's inability to get along without considerable reliance on others make the ministrations of others necessary and gratifying in terms of feeling secure. Awareness of infantile gratifications in dependency led in the early days of the use of psychological insights to the assumption that universally the human gets greater gratification from being dependent than from becoming independent; there was a phase in child rearing when it was thought that the child needed to be encouraged to learn, that he needed to be pushed into learning experiences, and that we should be wary of giving him much gratification in his infantile dependency lest he should enjoy it too much and be loath to relinquish it for his own efforts. *Today the impulse to learn – i.e. the impulse to gain self-sufficiency in order to feel safe – is recognized as a positive innate tendency.*

The infant soon reaches out for the spoon to feed himself. If permitted to experiment, he shows great gratification in his clumsy efforts and has a wonderful time hitting and missing his mouth and smearing himself with food. More usually, the busy mother

[1] *Ibid., loc. cit.*

who must conserve food, laundry, time and energy deprives him of this opportunity. Note, however, that when she takes the spoon he often resists and even yells with rage. Observe the young child's eager and persistent interest in learning to know the world about him – he reaches, he climbs, he touches, he feels, he grabs at everything within range. In the complexity of a civilized household he falls, he gets burned, he gets slapped to the tune of a continual 'NO, NO – Don't touch – Stop that!' It is small wonder, then, that he soon finds that learning is dangerous, that adults prefer to control him rather than permit him to manage his own life, and perhaps it is because early learning is fraught with so much restriction and disapproval that the enjoyment of helplessness seems to become the primary gratification in the lives of some children.

That the impulse to learn survives against so much discouragement is an argument for its strength and primacy. Why does it persist? Probably because *in the last analysis there is no real security, no deep assurance of survival in being wholly dependent on others. If one's security rests largely outside oneself one is forever uncertain.* This is a decisive point and one that has importance beyond the years of infancy and childhood. It is specially important for social workers. We deal largely with individuals at a time of enforced dependency or at a time when adverse circumstance has strengthened the impulses towards dependency, thus at the same time provoking anxiety about and resistance to the loss of self-dependence.

The child must have love as well as care
For the central issue of the child's life, the wish to be loved and to be cared for, the noteworthy point is that *he must have love as well as care* in order to feel secure and to develop a socialized self. Being completely dependent on adults for his survival, he fears loss of care and can only be assured of its continuance in so far as he is loved. This is one of the reasons why some children remain deeply insecure and anxious even though given excessive protective care. And strangely enough, these highly protective parents frequently overprotect their children because, not loving them enough to give unbegrudgingly, they need to deny their irritation and mask their wish to reject – i.e. to neglect the children – through enacting a role of great devotion. The children, however, sensing the lack of love, remain unsatisfied and insecure and manifest their resultant anxiety in behaviour disturbances of various sorts. In these situations a restless, demanding, attention-getting child who seems

insatiable in his need to be cared for is often encountered. Even though the gift without the giver is bare, he needs eternally to be given attention as an assurance that he is loved. His life may become an endless, restless quest.

Commonly also, these children, not having been loved sufficiently, grow into adults who have a meagre capacity to love others. One cannot give out of a vacuum; instead, one gives from a surplus. As unloved children become parents, they may repeat the pattern of their own parents. Frequently in their lives outside the family circle they are hostile, self-aggrandizing individuals who cannot relate themselves constructively to others and in positions of leadership may be driven by their irrational emotional needs into dictatorial measures. Or these children may solve their anxiety by becoming abjectly dependent, and their behaviour may be more submissive than aggressive, more self-condemning than openly hostile. The response patterns to the insecurity created by lack of love are varied; these two kinds of response are cited merely to establish the point that *when the child's need for love is frustrated in one way or another – i.e. when parents either show their lack of love through overt neglect or disguise it through overprotection – the chances for the attainment of rational attitudes and mature development are greatly diminished.*

The denial of love and care creates insecurity

In summary, then, we see that at the start of life all human beings need to be loved and cared for and to have an opportunity to learn in order to become increasingly less dependent on others. Dependence on others for love and care is the primary need, and in so far as this need is met freely the child reaches out spontaneously to learn to master his environment and is sustained in the failures and hurts that learning inevitably brings. This is a decisive point for all social workers in helping people, for it is important throughout the individual's life, and it is particularly significant for social workers because we deal with people at a time of defeat in the mastery of life's circumstances. In infancy and early childhood, denial of love and care creates deep insecurity as to the chances of survival and produces both anxiety and resentment. Frustration in opportunity to learn is likewise a threat to the impulse for survival and produces the same feelings, so that either or both lacks in the child's family life may well lead to behaviour disturbances.

Administrators will want to convey to workers the decisive

importance of adequate help in order that the physical welfare of the infant may be safeguarded. Economic security is important also from the standpoint that the mother, if anxious and harassed, transmits her disturbed feelings to the infant, perhaps to an even greater extent than when the child is older. The importance of the mother's care and, in the case of a mother who seeks advice in relation to working, the need for an adequate mother substitute who will give the infant or young child not only consistent care but also affectionate response, are obvious. A careful appraisal of the nature of the mother's relationship with the young child is needed in advising her as to whether she is wise to work outside the home. The significant points here are: Is there an adequate substitute for the mother? Will the added economic security the family gains through the mother's working and the satisfaction of being with other adults enable her to be a more calm and giving mother while with the child? Is her present attitude towards child care such that one questions her ability to afford the child a constructive relationship so that a mother substitute might be preferable?

THE SCHOOLCHILD NEEDS OPPORTUNITIES FOR CREATIVITY AND ATTAINMENT OF SKILLS

If his needs have been met during his earlier life so that his development is normal, the school-age child is less dependent, both physically and emotionally, on the adults in his environment than he was at an earlier age. At this point he experiences the first major separation from the security of the home and dependence on the parents, especially on the mother. In the early stage of this period he may seek to replace the parents with the schoolteacher and other parent substitutes, sometimes older children. In the interests of survival, the need to develop greater self-sufficiency emerges, perhaps to relieve anxiety caused by dependence on parent persons. He seeks security through close association with his own kind, children of the same age and sex, and tends to live in a group or gang that replaces the family to some extent. The group at this age denies both its dependence on parent persons and its attraction to the opposite sex. Symptomatic of these denials, one notes hostility towards the 'teacher's pet', the mother-dependent child, and aversion to petting and coddling except at a time of stress when there may be a momentary regression into the mother's arms. The noteworthy point about this age is that the child now spends the energy formerly used in his struggle for adaptation within the family in increasing his knowledge and acquiring physical strength and prowess. There is great gratification in creative activity and in games through which he develops skills and in the acquisition of knowledge through which he can come to be more self-sufficient. This is a period of preparation for the emancipation from parents that begins to take place in adolescence.

The schoolchild still needs his parents
Because of the child's strong denial, at this age, of dependency and because of his rejection of the opposite sex, we may assume a degree of self-sufficiency that is not there. He still needs his parents and at times of stress needs the mother very much. This is the age when the child wants to go out to play rather than to stay at home, but on returning is reassured to find the mother there at least some of the time. An empty house occasioned by the mother's working, parents who are anxious and disturbed over the economic situation, an unemployed father who is depressed and defeated by a too-competitive world, do not give these children the base of security that they still need to sustain them in their struggle to make their place in the group.

In this period, the child whose dependency needs are not being met and have not been met in the earlier years, may cling to the parents and be fearful of the give-and-take of the group. If he moves out into the group, his fears may make him the brunt of other children's aggressions or his hostilities may bring him into open conflict and win so much opposition that he is driven back into dependence on adults and into playing with younger children. If at this age he does not have adequate opportunity for developing his mental and physical potentialities, if he does not have opportunities for creative activity, he may readily resort to destructive activities. In either instance, whether he solves his problem through choice of unwholesome activity that gets him into trouble or through clinging to the ways of his earlier years, he is not developing the resources for mastering his environment that are the basis for the inner security essential to stability in adult life.

If the child's previous experience has met his needs, his early school years are a period during which there are relatively few problems. He is an easy person, provided he has the opportunity for lots of play and plenty of chance for pursuit of intellectual and physical interests that will stimulate growth and give him that feeling of adequacy and self-sufficiency for which he is striving. At this period, difficulties are avoided if emotionally demanding relationships are not forced on him, such as too much maternal affection centring on the boy or too much paternal affection centring on the girl. Too much parental control and repression are also inadvisable. Children living in crowded cities often have a more difficult time than those living in the country or in small communities where the mischievous activity normal to this age is less likely to get the child into trouble. The more repressive the environment at this period, the more chance of disturbing the child.

Through the very fact of poor economic circumstances, schoolchildren in poor families may lack the opportunities essential for development. They may lack the stabilizing care of parents who are not too driven by the pressures of life to meet the dependency needs of their children. Instead, these overburdened parents may be inclined to slough them off now that they are becoming physically competent to fend for themselves. Social workers need to understand the potentialities of this age period. Planning with parents should be based on an understanding of the needs of the child – both those that may be met within the home and those that may be met by the parents through effective use of community resources. When mothers seek help in deciding whether they will work and leave children of this age relatively unsupervised, there should be careful appraisal of the child's self-sufficiency, the mother's capacity to meet his need if she stays at home, and community resources that may be used in the interests of his development. In their work with the community, workers with understanding of children's needs will more convincingly present the importance of adequate services. When insufficient agency funds or restrictive community attitudes are factors in forcing mothers whose children need their major attention to seek employment, this is especially significant.

THE ADOLESCENT IS ALL AGES IN ONE

Adolescence has been described as a period in which all the earlier needs and phases of life are relived in some measure and in which certain early conflicts – those of dependency and authority and those pertaining to sex – are revived and lived through in the process of a general reorganization of the personality. The child will have a difficult adolescence, therefore, if he had a difficult early life experience that prevented him from being emotionally free to develop his self-dependence to the utmost. Furthermore, his capacity for sublimation of the now active sexual impulses is attained through the acquisition of knowledge, skill and strength. *Also, if the child has known more deprivation than gratification in relationships so that he has had to invest his love largely or wholly in himself and is basically self-aggrandizing and fearful in relation to others, he will have an especially difficult time at adolescence.*

The adolescent must be allowed childish behaviour in times of stress
For the child whose earlier years have been essentially normal, adolescence still is a period of some conflict in which there will be discomfort for him as well as for those who live with him. It is a time when he reaches out to find self-realization in more adult ways and as a natural protective impulse resorts comfortably to the gratifications of childhood when he finds the adult role too frustrating or too threatening. That is, when his efforts at self-dependency fail or become too difficult, he may revert momentarily to episodes of childish behaviour and resorts to the interests and activities of childhood. *It is important that this child-adult, i.e. the adolescent, should be permitted his childish ways at moments of tension, and it is a wise parent or social worker who encourages the adult impulses and eases the anxieties that the reality demands of the adult world momentarily engender, while at the same time permitting him recourse to childish ways when he needs protection from that world in which he has not yet found a secure place.*

These fragmentary regressions may serve a twofold purpose: (*a*) they permit him to meet needs formerly unmet and to work through earlier conflicts, and (*b*) they enable him to use the old familiar ways as a needed balm, solace and protection at moments of hurt or defeat when he has found the adult world too much for him. Often adults fail to realize the usefulness of the old childish ways and are condemning and punitive because of their fear that the child is not developing properly and their concern that seemingly he is never going to grow up. They can comprehend the child. Adult behaviour may also be within their scope of understanding, but this child-adult, this bundle of contradictions who is momentarily one age and momentarily another, is a strain on their powers of adaptation.

The child who has grown rapidly, i.e. shot up physically almost overnight, is commonly encountered. Undue demands may be made on him. Overnight, parents, teachers and others expect adult judgement from this adult frame and may suddenly become intolerant of momentary relapses into childish behaviour, gusts of temper, wide mood swings in which undue optimism or undue pessimism occur. They begin to impose adult demands and to condemn childish impulses, thus increasing insecurity and the need to be childish. Such an adolescent has a difficult time. He has no real place in either world.

Another situation frequently met is that in which parents are gratified by the child's dependence and threatened by his adult behaviour. They encourage the childish behaviour and combat the child's self-assertion. Reacting with alarm to his growing independence, they sometimes feel it is a rejection of themselves. These parents enhance the safety and comfort of childhood and unconsciously encourage its continuance. Later, these same parents may suddenly find the child objectionable and abruptly reject their self-created infant, thus putting him completely to rout by demanding sudden change. The gist of the situation is that in this period of reorganization and transition, the adolescent is normally a bundle of contradictions. It is as though, before giving up the various stages of childhood, he must relive them or momentarily retreat to them.

Sex identity is in a state of flux

The adolescent is, therefore, all ages in one. For example, in his sex life, he is momentarily self-loving; at another moment hero worshipping individuals of the same sex; again, he is momentarily strongly attracted to persons of the opposite sex. His sex identity is in a state of flux, not yet crystallized in any one form but expressed variously. This self-love is shown in his urge for self-adornment and absorption in 'looks'. The adolescent will spend hours before the mirror; bodily interest and concern are very great. His impulses towards his own sex are shown in hero-worship and 'crushes'. He may retreat from spasmodic interest in the opposite sex to his own sex, particularly after any defeat in relationship with the opposite sex, and at such times his hatred of the other sex may become pronounced. His normal attraction to the opposite sex needs no elaboration. The popular terms 'girl crazy' and 'boy crazy' indicate the intensity and instability of many of these early relationships. Success or failure – i.e. gratification or hurt in the first venture – may become a determinant of future experience, and therefore the relationships of a young person at this stage of development are most important. His eventual sex development has been predisposed towards final crystallization in one form or another by the nature of his relationships with his parents. Since, however, his sex identity is not yet formed, these adolescent love relationships may be decisive.

At this age, general social adjustment may show the same two-way pull. The individual may need to be momentarily the lone wolf, going off by himself. A very real purpose may be served by self-imposed isolation, provided it is not prolonged. Or momentarily he may need to gang up with his own sex against the opposite sex. During these phases, there will be great emphasis on likeness to others. He must wear the same clothes, think and act the same way, possess the same gadgets. Hostility towards those who are different may again be pronounced, as during the earlier gang age. The young person's gropings for individuality may also undergo phases of overemphasis. His need to stress his individuality may take bizarre forms in dress, in conspicuous behaviour, in unrealistic, independent action wherein he will 'die' for some trifling cause or outreach himself in defending those who depart from the group. Normally, as adolescence proceeds, the person seems increasingly gratified with activities in mixed groups, more responsive to the needs of others, more altruistic, more stable in his choices, and more realistic in his strivings.

The adolescent wavers between reverting to childhood and striving for adulthood
What importance has this for social workers? Obviously, many of the so-called problems of adolescence can be regarded as normal growing pains. If we see them in this light, rather than as problems we will focus on providing opportunities for growth rather than on direct correction of the behaviour manifestations. *Behaviour at this age might be classified into two groups: (a) that which shows the wish to remain a child, and (b) that which shows the desire for adulthood and is problematic in that lack of adequacy as an adult may drive the young person to outreach himself in pretending to be more adult than he is.* This striving may take the form of undertaking work beyond his years, seeking sophisticated recreational outlets, and seeking mature sex life of an uncertain nature at an early age. In striving beyond himself, he runs the chance of frustration, defeat and hurts of many sorts. In general, we help the adolescent most when we grant him the right still to resort to some childish behaviour. Condemnation of such behaviour should be avoided whenever possible. However,

it is well recognized by those who have had wide experience in helping adolescents that frequently they need definite guidance and supportive judgements as to the right way of doing things; preferably this should come from someone they admire and respect. It has been said that fear of insecurity, present in children of all ages, becomes at adolescence an anxiety about the future, in which schooling, career and marriage are absorbing concerns.

Planning for the future may have a stabilizing effect
We help the adolescent most, then, when we help him to make reasonable plans for the future and at the same time help him to obtain opportunities in the present for their eventual realization. Expert vocational guidance is most important at this age, and workers should make every effort to explain to the family the use of such community resources. Clinics available to child welfare services might well be used more often to determine the abilities of children rather than so predominantly for help with learning disabilities and behaviour problems.

Knowledge of the mental capacity and aptitudes of the adolescent is highly important if he is to be educated suitably. Appropriate education is essential to his general social adjustment.

Decisions regarding work and continued education are important issues with which the adolescent frequently needs help. Because of his tendency to outreach himself, his choice will not necessarily be wise. He needs the protection of rigidly imposed child-labour laws and wise counselling about his educational goals. *When the future becomes particularly uncertain, the adolescent can be expected to respond with anxiety, expressed in behaviour disturbances.*

Adolescents in poor families may be subjected to special stresses
Adolescents in families who are living precariously from an economic standpoint are subjected to certain special stresses. Frequently more adult demands are placed on them at an early age. Opportunities to plan for the future are more meagre and the future itself has greater uncertainties than in the economically secure family. Frequently also, the parents, anxious, uncertain, defeated because they have found the world a too-competitive arena, convey their insecurity to the child. And so we might expect the children in this age group in many poor families to present greater problems in emancipation. They may well cling more tenaciously to the parents or, in the interest of survival, be compelled to escape the

uncertainties of their family life through an abrupt and premature 'cutting off'. They may *needfully* assert their right to keep their own earnings and out of a tragic necessity pursue their own paths unhampered by the burdens of the past.

The worker may need to understand the individual's need for survival apart from the family as something other than a selfishness that is to be condemned and opposed. Young people in economically disadvantaged families may need and seek supportive help in finding and making the most of present opportunities and planning realistically for the future. Such vital issues as the young person leaving home are sometimes at stake. Parents raise difficult questions about their problem in either guiding or coercing their earning children to spend their money properly. Because of this, it seems advisable to give rather full consideration to the meaning of money to adolescents. We should probably find that frequently it still has some of the same meanings for adults.

MONEY HAS GREAT EMOTIONAL SIGNIFICANCE

Money means different things to different people at different ages. For children, money normally takes on meaning in terms of the significance it has within the family. In adolescence one may find either conformity to the family pattern in handling money or a strong reaction against it. Some children learn good money habits within the family and some bad habits, but the handling of money is not as simple as that. *Money is an infinitely complex subject. It has great emotional significance, and the meaning money has for the individual will determine what he will do with it.* Within our society money has been the symbol of adequacy, even of worth. It wins respect for the individual. To be rich sometimes is to be both powerful and wise. To be rich frequently is to be forgiven many sins of omission and commission.

Money may have affectional significance
Within the family, money has had great affectional value. When a child is bad, allowances have been withheld; when good, money and things are given. Likewise, when parents are feeling good, they may give freely; when they are out of sorts, they may withhold the pennies. Children soon tend to reach out for money as an assurance of love. Beside the very gratifying things it buys to compensate for life's deprivations, it assures one of being loved.

This use of money as an expression of negative or positive feeling may permeate family life. Father comes home and has a tantrum because mother has overspent their funds. Mother, almost unconsciously, may have overspent because she was depressed. She was depressed because tensions have been acute between her and her husband. Father is anxious and worried because the demands of the family have become oppressive. Mother knows intellectually that he no longer freely gives her either money or love because of harsh realities, but emotionally she needs to be loved and when frustrated her old childish need for money as reassurance is activated. So she spends. Father has a temper tantrum; mother feels all the more unloved and hostile, with perhaps an increased need to spend, and so the pernicious circle is established. Children soon sense the affectional values money has in the parental relationship. Father gets a rise; mother loves him for it. Father feels expansive and gives freely to mother and the children, not merely because he has the money to give but because now he has the love to give. And so the child's need for and use of money is strongly interfused with affectional need. In this he is frequently expressing his gratifications, deprivations and conflicts, and is working through much that is important to him.

Money may be a symbol of power
Money has other meanings also. *To many it is a symbol of power and strength, a symbol of the adequacy of the adult.* In the social group this value is pronounced. Early on the child gets the feeling that adults have money – at least they control whatever money there is. So the child begins to feel, 'When I get big, I will have money too and I will control it.' In some instances, complete control will be expressed in wild spending as an exhibition to others or as an assurance to oneself of one's adult adequacy. For other children, doing 'as I please' with money – i.e. control of it – will mean hanging on to it, keeping it all to himself with the illusion that the more money he has, the bigger and more adequate he is. The deeply anxious, unloved child who tends to withdraw into himself may react in this way. Or the deeply dependent, insecure child may anxiously and willingly give it all to his mother. Therefore, the little hoarder – the child about whom the parents, teachers and caseworkers are less anxious in regard to money – may not have more mental health than his spendthrift brother; he may sometimes have even less mental health. What this means is that children are frequently expressing

their growth, their impulses towards adulthood, in their combat for money and their use of it. They are working through much in relation to parents and parent persons in their assertion of the right to do with it as they please. When we realize these meanings, we see the importance of understanding what money means to each person. We may then be less anxious about his practices and hope-fully more understanding of how he feels when he must meet the (to him) coercive reality of only having enough for essentials.

Adult judgement about money cannot be expected from adolescents
As might be expected from all that has been said about normal adolescence, certainly adolescents cannot be expected to use adult judgement about money. We must expect unevenness. The young person may seem to be developing some stability and judgement about this when, all at once, there may be a relapse into childish attitudes and habits when some compelling need takes possession of him. Take for example, two young people in families receiving social security benefits.

(i) Jim, aged sixteen, had been earning money doing chores after school. For two years he had been planning consistently, spending a little on fun, a little for things of substance, and saving some for a technical school course in which his hopes were centred. Suddenly in one week-end he spent two years' savings. His aspiring mother, reduced to tears, berated him. She failed to see the connection between the spending spree and the boy's disappointment at not getting into the football team and his anxiety over his resultant status with his girl friend.

(ii) Paul, aged fifteen, had also earned and saved some money for a technical training course. Intellectually precocious and physically frail, this youngster had led an isolated life with academic achievement his only goal and source of security. Again, an aspiring mother was reduced to tears when a box arrived containing physical training equipment for which all his savings had been expended.

Attitudes towards money are symptomatic of basic individual needs
Money may buy many gratifying material things. It buys new and exciting experiences, one of which may be the longed-for emancipa-tion from the parents. It may even buy friends, and the adolescent

cannot be expected to discern that friendship that has been bought is a poor purchase. Beneath these externals money may buy for the child a sense of security, of belonging, of being loved, adequate, even powerful. Again we must remember that the adolescent's attitudes towards the use of money are symptomatic of basic individual needs within the framework of needs peculiar to his age period. His childish impulses in relation to money are again serving a twofold purpose: (a) he is working through many conflicts unresolved in the past, and (b) he is reverting to old familiar ways as a needed respite from the harsh reality of the adult world of which he is not yet an integral part. From our adult point of view, what may seem to be random, purposeless spending may be serving an important purpose. Frequently adolescents in some of their seemingly unwise spending actually are, like Paul, putting first things first – they are always revealing their need, i.e. telling us much about themselves. Certainly it is through earning and spending, through the management and mismanagement of funds, that the young person may meet certain basic needs and thus realize growth. Only in this way can he learn the value of money and how to manage it. Money management, therefore, is not related solely to intellect, training and experience. If the child goes into adulthood with many childish needs unmet, then the distorted personality may continue to be manifested in this area of his life as in other areas.

Problems arise with wage-earning children in families living on social security
Young people in families on social security are denied to a greater extent than children in most other families the self-determining use of money described above. Although they too may be working through many conflicts unresolved in the past and may also be reverting to childish ways as a needed respite from the harsh reality of the adult world, they are often confronted with the demands of the adult world as imposed by the level of social security benefits. This is not necessarily a destructive experience. While other children may have had less deprivation and with their first earnings may now have more freedom to do as they wish with some of the money, still the helpful parent, while permitting some freedom, has also been stimulating gradual assumption of adult attitudes through encouraging both saving and contributing to others. This has been made gratifying in various ways, notably through helping the youngster to plan for the future and through according him greater

recognition in general as an adult. The greater problem in the family on social security frequently lies in the fact that the whole process has been much less gradual. The youngster has had little money in the past, and when he suddenly gets some, he does not have time to find himself in relation to it but is expected immediately to use it for his ordinary unexciting needs. Furthermore, these young people frequently have not had the stabilizing influence of planning for the future.

In such families as elsewhere, the reaction of the young person to earning and spending will reflect the nature of his family life in varied ways. When the individual's affectional needs have been met in childhood and when his family relationships are essentially good, even though certain adolescent dependency and authority conflicts may now be present, his initial protest against restricted use of his money may quickly subside. It is important in these instances that the young person's resentments over denial should be understood, and that any deprivations should be acknowledged. When this is done, he may move towards taking over responsibility, especially if he attains recognition and status by so doing.

Parents may be helped to see the need to give a wage-earning child a greater part in financial planning, more place in the family councils, and more freedom in other aspects of his life.

(i) In one family where James, a sixteen-year-old boy, was working and contributing resentfully to the family budget, the worker learned in talking matters over with him that his resentment stemmed primarily from being treated like a child at the same time that adult demands were being imposed in regard to money. The mother had unwittingly not recognized the more grown-up status to which his years and earnings entitled him. Furthermore, because of her own economic deprivation and financial worry, she had tried to seize possessively on his earnings and from her fears of the future had tried anxiously to dictate all the spending. Fortunately, in this instance the mother was able to modify her handling of the situation and the youngster quickly assumed more adult attitudes with considerable gratification in his new status.

(ii) In contrast to James, we see a different situation in the case of John P, aged eighteen, another eldest boy in a family receiving social security benefit. John's mother anxiously turned to the worker for help in prevailing on John not to leave home. To his mother, John seemed selfish and ungrateful in wanting to keep his total earnings to spend in his own way and threatening to move out and pay for lodgings elsewhere rather than pay for this at home. He was unresponsive to the worker's ill-advised efforts to help him to see that he would be losing money by moving, as well as to his appeals to his obligation to his mother and his disabled father. In several discussions it became clear that his attitude was an expression of a strong desire to leave home, where he was entangled in an old attachment to a dominating mother and where he suffered the continual hostile rivalry of his father. Bringing money home had intensified this conflict to such an extent that recently he had solved the problem by staying away from home as much as possible and by squandering his money, behaviour that pleased the father, who had done likewise in his wage-earning days. It won the mother's condemnation, however, and her continual comparison of him with his father, which both irritated and gratified him. At least he could reassure himself that he was now a man. A shift had occurred in the family align-ments when he became a wage earner. Whereas formerly mother and son had seemingly sided together against the father, now father and son were aligned against the mother.

In view of the limitations of his life situation, the construc-tive course of action for this youth was clearly his own plan for himself, that of withdrawing from the family and of assuming full support of himself. He was caught in a conflict which he could ease only in destructive ways if he remained in the home. In the interests of self-survival, he was using his money and the issue with the agency as a means to emanci-pate himself. The worker could not see the relatively con-structive meaning of this action but considered it bad for him, in the long run, to be permitted to be so selfish. In his opinion it would be better if somehow John could be persuasively coerced into staying at home, where, in doing his part, he might develop more mature attitudes. The worker was powerless to keep him there and so saw him go with a great sense of personal failure.

We can sympathize with the worker's concern over some of the circumstances under which John P left home. The dependencies and hostilities involved in an unfriendly break may not be a sound basis for real emancipation. They may well go with him to be lived out in other relationships in self-frustrating ways. And yet, in order to survive he may *have* to leave. How much he may grow through the separation cannot be predicted.

The problem of the young person who is earning is widespread, and many examples could be cited to show the difficulties presented. Community attitudes as well as housing shortages create pressure to keep the young person within his own family, obstructing establishment of a family of his own or going forward into any life plan he may make for himself. Unless he is unusually mature, his social adjustment and general personality growth may suffer. On encountering such cases, workers may get caught in the conflict between the individual's welfare and community attitudes. They may identify with the young person or the community. They may resort to moral judgements because they see the youth as irresponsible or ungrateful. They may fail to see that he is struggling to take responsibility for himself, commonly a prerequisite to assuming it for others. In either instance, they may fail to understand the youth's own conflict, for he may be torn between wishing to go forth to a life of his own and feeling his obligation to remain. When caught in the conflict, one way or another, the worker may fail to be helpful, as in the case of John.

Young people's attitudes towards money reflect social problems
Repeatedly, social workers express concern over self-aggrandizing attitudes evidenced by young people who are prematurely earning 'big money'. This manifestation may well be a commentary on the lacks in many lives. It must be remembered that *we can expect mature attitudes towards money and enlightened use of it only in the adolescent who does not have too much at stake emotionally in earning and spending.* When he has many deprivations for which to compensate, deep conflicts to appease, and great frustration to ease, he may be driven to meet his own compelling needs without reference to others. He may have small capacity to endure denial and, therefore, may be unable to postpone until tomorrow the gratifications money will buy for him today. In these cases there is not so much a money problem as the reflection of many profound social problems, which, belatedly, we may be unable to help the individual to solve. The

children of tomorrow are another matter. These young people today point to the need for broad social and economic measures to safeguard family life in order that more mature personalities may gradually emerge.

When we are called on to advise in such problems as those cited above, it is important that we should understand the meaning of money to the specific individual. How many workers gain this understanding? The young person will frequently not be able to put into words precisely what money means to him. Therefore we must derive the meaning from an array of factors such as the character of his relationships with his parents and their attitudes towards money in general as well as towards his money, the character of his relationships with his brothers and sisters, rivalries in which the individual feels outdone, and his status in school and social life. Is he doing well in school or failing? Is he physically adequate in competitive games? Is he accepted or rejected by his social group? How does he spend his money? For what? And on whom? These are all important questions in determining what he is striving to get other than the actual material goods or pleasures in and of themselves.

Money is significant for the total personality
When we consider the value of money for the individual, adult or child, when we realize that it is important to the total personality in relation to the life situation at any given time, then perhaps we will bring more understanding to the administration of social services. In the light of this understanding perhaps we will appreciate, even more than previously, the wisdom in general of safeguarding for the individual his customary freedom and responsibility in the use of money.

Most people will experience some genuine security in that they have a continued opportunity to plan and manage their own lives within the limits set by meagre grants. There will be some individuals who, unable to plan or manage resourcefully, will build up resentment unless they receive more help through additional services. They may want and need additional help in budgeting and planning so that they may experience a feeling of adequacy rather than failure with resultant insecurity. In so far as benefits are inadequate, this situation can be expected to occur with greater frequency. The problem then arises of giving such help without conveying the impression that we are dictating the use of the money. This may involve clarifying repeatedly with the recipient the fact that he has a right to this help and that it is for him to use it as he wishes.

We place a great deal of emphasis on the individual's *right* to social security in the beliefs that it dignifies, that it frees him from humiliation, and that it leaves him unshackled by feelings of personal obligation to the agency, all elements that should operate against the production of dependency. In the light of our understanding of the emotional meaning that money has for people, we will realize that the values of such a right may be greatly undermined for many persons when benefits are inadequate. *Many individuals who have repeatedly met eligibility requirements are more impressed with the deprivation than with the right, if they are continuously entitled to less than they need.* For many people, to be deprived is to be humiliated. Humiliation evokes resentment, and feelings of resentment in turn engender feelings of heavy obligation when these feelings occur in a relationship in which the individual is being accorded his right to survive. It may seem strange to many of us that feelings of resentment can evoke excessive feelings of obligation. Perhaps it may seem less strange if we can recall a time when we ourselves had to take something from someone we did not like or from someone who gave, begrudgingly, less than we needed. Perhaps we may recall that we felt under a greater obligation in these instances than to persons who helped us generously, freely and unquestioningly.

What happens between individuals may happen between an individual and an agency. We have ample evidence that clients do personalize agencies, the agency's wishes to the contrary. In spite of the concept that the public agency is not a person who gives or withholds but instead an agency that respects the right to which every citizen is impartially entitled, the agency may well represent to the client 'that worker up there who gives too little and asks questions with tiresome regularity'. He may come to feel that he is given to begrudgingly and with great question. The resultant sense of undue obligation places him in the defensive position of an individual with a debt he cannot pay, thus leaving him humiliated and helpless. When we realize this, we see how important it is that workers should apply this understanding of individuals so that the individual's feelings about his stress will be understood. We also see the importance of bending every effort towards the attainment of adequate payments if social security provisions are to achieve their constructive purpose.

4

ADULTHOOD AND OLD AGE

Among other factors, physical self-dependence is important in giving the adult greater security than the child. A significant factor in the social structure within which social workers help people, however, is the fact that man does not have full use of this biological capacity for survival. To be sure, he may be able to survive alone on an island abounding in natural resources. However, he has much less chance for survival alone in modern society, for the goods that surround him are not his for the taking. *Therefore, unless broad social security provisions are made available to man as his inalienable right to survival, he may be doomed to continue in the psychological state of childhood, anxiously dependent on others, insecure, and unfree to move courageously into full assumption of adult responsibilities. This may result in the continuance of self-aggrandizing strivings and the persistence of irrational behaviour.* Social security provision is a basic requirement for the development of the mature personality, a state of being essential if democracy as a way of life is to be realized in full measure.

If the adult's basic needs have been met fairly adequately throughout infancy, childhood and adolescence so that growth towards maturity has been realized normally, then he will inevitably have needs and wants beyond the mere privilege of survival. He will have ambitions, an urge for accomplishment, a desire for participation in group life, an impulse to give and live beyond himself in many ways. If circumstances deny him the opportunity to work and to realize some of these aspirations, if they limit his relationships in the family and the community, he may be deeply frustrated and experience a hunger equivalent to actual physical hunger. Man cannot live by bread alone.

Social workers have come to know the emotionally starved adult and to recognize some of the ways in which commonly he appeases that hunger. Frequently they are not constructive ways. To the inexperienced social worker they may seem quite irrational.

F

To the social worker whose knowledge and experience enable him to see the *meaning of behaviour*, these 'unwise' solutions take on a wisdom of their own. The parent who buys his toddler a pink elephant instead of the shoes the child needs; the harassed and over-burdened mother who periodically falls ill and obviously takes pleasure in clinic visits and hospital care (in one such instance, the woman commented enthusiastically to her worker as she was being returned to the hospital, 'The doctors and nurses there are the nicest people I've ever known'); the parent who, living vicariously in the accomplishments of his children, makes demands on them beyond their years; the unemployed man who takes to the tavern – all these reactions have been known in individual instances to bespeak potentials for a healthier life that have been frustrated.

THE EMOTIONALLY MATURE ADULT

In general, there are two major concerns about the needs of the adult – preparation for work that will assure survival, and the attainment of some degree of social productivity. On reaching maturity, the individual's energies will be concerned largely with the struggle for existence, but he will be concerned also with the establishment and maintenance of family life and with other creative activity or socially productive work that contributes to the life of the group. Effective fulfilment of these needs will depend largely on the nature of the relationships the individual is able to establish and maintain and on the meaning of these relationships to himself and others. It will depend also on opportunities to continue to learn. Since the course of life can be described as a continuous process of learning, i.e. of adaptation to ever-changing external and internal conditions, the need for opportunity to understand and learn to meet the changing factors and forces of life is ever present. The need to be loved and cared for, the central issue of the young child's life, continues but becomes less self-centred. In so far as the individual builds up a surplus through having been loved adequately, an impulse and capacity to love others develops.

That largely hypothetical person, an emotionally mature adult, defies a precise descriptive definition. Perhaps certain character-istics of what we mean by 'maturity' might be stated roughly as those of *a person in whom enjoyment of dependence or inordinate pride in independence is replaced by gratification in interdependence. He still has a considerable need to depend on others, a need to be loved and a need to be cared for at such times and in those areas of his life in which he is unable to care for himself. He has a need also to have an opportunity to care for himself and to contribute to the welfare of others.* Growth from infancy to adulthood may be described as a process of change in which the individual moves from loving the world as part of himself to loving, i.e. respecting, himself as part of the world. In so far as the individual is basically secure through having experienced relationships in which he has been adequately loved and through having experienced opportunities for maximum development of his mental and physical capacities, his emancipation from his parents will have occurred naturally, gradually and completely. He will, therefore, have little anxiety about either his need to depend on others or his need to compete with others, i.e. his wish to excel others.

Mature people can be distinguished through the way they use their right to services

Social workers have learned, through experience, what at first seemed a strange contradiction to the traditional ideas in which we had been reared, namely, that *it is the relatively secure adult with considerable strength and capacity for independence who becomes least anxious, least resentful and least humiliated when through force of circumstance he turns to others for help.* This is not to say that he has no discomfort in asking for help even when it is clear to him that this help is a right to which he is entitled. In our society, in which most adults today have been reared in the ideology that self-support and self-respect are synonymous, even the most secure adult may experience some feelings of inadequacy in relation to this ideal. Even he may feel some strangeness and uncertainty and loss of adequacy in that he has been unable to cope with circumstance. His anxiety, however, will be more readily allayed through our attitude. He will more readily than others take hold of the idea of 'right' and use it to ease his own hurt feelings. He will be less prone to slump into prolonged dependency and, therefore, less fearful and protesting or less resentful and critical of what we provide for him. He will be more likely to participate actively in discussion about his need for a service and in general will continue to be active in handling his affairs. He will be less prone to carry over the disturbed feelings in this experience into other life relationships, like the man who responds to loss of status as a wage earner in the home by becoming hostile and competing with his children for the attention of his wife.

How the worker feels about dependency is important
The worker who has little respect for the person who is in economic straits, or in need of some other social service, who does not have a conviction of the person's right to agency provisions, and who therefore distrusts the applicant and is more intent on proving his ineligibility than determining his eligibility, will question provocatively rather than respectfully. This intensifies the applicant's discomfort and tends to lower his morale. Unless the client has unusual inner strength, he may experience a threat to his adequacy resulting sometimes in a regressive response in his relationship with the agency. When a worker has such attitudes to helping the individual to establish his right to services, they operate against his constructive use of agency's services, which could contribute to the strengthening of self-dependence and a diminishing need for the agency's support.

Most individuals feel some discomfort in applying for and receiving services
Social workers deal with relatively few so-called 'mature adults'. Many people only approximate to this state. Because of frustrations experienced in childhood relationships and the obstacles to full realization of mental and physical capacities many people carry into adulthood vestiges of their childhood selves. Most, however, manage to get along fairly adequately. The people served by the social services are frequently those whose adverse life circumstances have been exceptionally frustrating and whose relationships have suffered the strain of limiting life conditions. More often than not, therefore, workers encounter disturbed feelings symptomatic of profound discomfort when major catastrophes of life drive these people to others for help. They too, however, often have had considerable capacity to get along in adequate fashion, and that capacity may be restored as present strains are eased if early frustrations have not been profoundly damaging.

Even though our conception is that we proffer social services as both a right and a helpful service, many people will be inclined to feel dependent and to assign to the agency the identity of helper. Lifelong insecurities will render them anxious. Lifelong feelings of inadequacy may be the basis for feelings of humiliation. Lifelong feelings of resentment stemming from deprivation, frustration and humiliation will be intensified and may well be directed towards those on whom they are now forced by circumstance to depend.

Furthermore, many problems other than the need for a specific service will frequently be exerting pressure in this relationship with the agency that proffers help in at least one area.

The anxiety of these people, therefore, may not be easy to allay. They may not take hold readily of the idea of *right* to ease their own discomfort. Instead, that very discomfort may find expression in varied ways, depending on the meaning of the present need in relation to old failures, former conflicts, frustrations in relationships, and previous sources of security or insecurity. They may be more inclined to relapse into dependency, less free to use a service, with many anxieties about and resistance to agency demands. Fearful of their own impulses towards dependency, they may be full of protests about the service, resentful and critical of what is done or not done for them. Conversely, they may react with abject gratitude and feelings of obligation that reinforce the original feelings of helplessness and operate against resumption of activity in their affairs. As previously indicated, they may tend to carry over the disturbed feelings in this experience into other life relationships. How services are rendered becomes important. The extent to which we can offer them a helping experience that restores self-respect through giving them as much command of the situation as they can assume is decisive.

Offer services as a right with no obligation to accept them
Any given service must be proffered as a right to which clients are entitled but which they are not obliged to use. Because humans tend to react to any one phase of an agency experience in terms of the total self and in terms of a totality of need, it may not be a simple matter to render services clearly distinguished one from another. An agency may conveniently divide itself into different services and proffer them like different commodities. But a man has not two separate sides to his head or his heart. Therefore, regardless of an agency's particular conception of its service, the administration of an individual's right to help at times of need in some instances may be identified in his feelings as an understanding readiness to see and meet his various needs.

In other instances, the person's resentment over taking help in any form may be intensified by the offer of additional help. He may want the help in the objective interests of himself and his family. At the same time, he may not want the help in the subjective interests of his self-esteem. Or the desire for help may be the dominant impulse, so he does not refuse it. This is a decisive differentiation that should serve as a guide to use in our subsequent efforts. If he accepts the help, his discomfort may not be allayed readily by our interpretations of right and freedom of choice, and he may need to use his feelings of obligation resentfully against us. We then encounter responses that say in word or act, 'because you got me this service I have to depend on you in general'. *In such instances we should focus on understanding his resentment and easing it with the hope of reconciling the two facets of his need – i.e. taking help and maintaining self-esteem.*

Work is important to the adult
The importance of work in the life of the adult is well recognized. It is commonly agreed that work is 'good for people' and that in idleness man deteriorates in one way or another. The conflicting impulses towards regression and progression persistent in some measure throughout life may have led to the puritanical assumption that because work is good for man he has a disinclination for it and, conversely, because idleness is bad for him it is highly desirable to him. If this is so, it is indeed a sad commentary on the mental health of great masses of people.

Based on observations made in the study and treatment of humans, the student of human behaviour has a strong conviction that *normally* the adult wants to work, that he has an imperative need to work, and that he is deeply frustrated in his growth impulses when denied that opportunity. Furthermore, *it is not idleness itself but the frustration in idleness that sets in operation the regressive process through which men break down or become what is commonly termed 'pauperized'.* As social workers increasingly comprehend this fact they will have more faith in the client's willingness to work.

Persons who are physically, mentally and emotionally disabled and hence unemployable may include some legendary instances of pauperization. A careful study of the background of these people may give a better understanding of this condition. Employability from the standpoint of physical fitness is sometimes carefully determined by medical examinations. When physical unfitness has been ruled out, an individual's disinclination for work, continued complaints of physical symptoms, ineffectual attempts to get or hold jobs, any or all of these manifestations are commonly diagnosed by lay staff under some such nomenclature as 'work-shy', 'malingering' and so on. Until it is recognized that man normally wants to work and that disinclination for work may well be a symptom of mental or emotional illness, available psychiatric services will not be utilized for the study and treatment of this condition. Until this is done, we may fail to be helpful to persons who might be helped and we may treat unjustly those who are incurably ill.

In this connection, it is recognized that lack of psychiatric services may be an obstacle to the determination of employability on a mental-emotional basis. Use of these resources when available may throw valuable light on the problem of the 'work-shy' individual.

THE ESTABLISHMENT OF A FAMILY IS CRUCIAL

As the adult establishes and endeavours to maintain a family, the success of the venture will depend in large measure on the extent to which he is no longer immersed in a self-centred struggle to meet his own needs but has instead some 'surplus' to spend outside himself. The stability of his family life will also depend on chance factors and on the extent to which limitations in his capacity for relationship are balanced by his partner's capacity to give. Affectional and economic deprivation in her earlier years may lead a woman to show in marriage a childlike need to be loved and cared for. Her husband may be able to meet her excessive need as long as he is feeling adequate, for instance through having satisfactory work, so that he has status as head of the family and status in the community as a wage earner. Some of the gaps in the relationship may have been filled and the marriage sustained through his ability to provide for his wife. Loss of satisfying work and the loss of status entailed in unemployment may, however, create feelings of inadequacy in the husband that make him temporarily dependent on his wife for assurance of love. Unable to meet his affectional need, she may be irritated, particularly when he is showing less affection and providing so little financially. She is even less able than usual to meet his need. And so mutual frustration may lead to a breakdown in a relationship that might have continued had not changing circumstances brought a shift in the balance of needs.

The arrival of children is a crucial test of the maturity of the parents and the stability of the marriage relationship. Social workers have long been familiar with the father who deserts, turns to drink, or in other ways becomes irresponsible and hostile at the birth of a child. They are also familiar with the mother who is irritated beyond endurance and whose resentment and anxiety over having to meet demands beyond her capacity are expressed in various ways, such as discouragement, self-pity, depression, overt display of temper, nagging, erratic discipline, poor management, neglect, or excessive efforts to outreach her scope. Even under advantageous circumstances, the complete dependency of infants and the prolonged demands of children make parenthood a responsibility that is generally carried with ease and enjoyment only by those whose life relationships have given them the capacity to meet the needs of others freely and flexibly. When an individual has this capacity, he is not only able to meet the dependency needs of the children but also – because he does not need to realize his own frustrated self in them – is able to grant them self-identity and release them for growth towards independence. Since most individuals bring vestiges of childish need into marriage and parenthood, some problems are normally found in parent-child relationships.

Economic insecurity heightens the stress of parenthood
It is generally agreed that lack of basic economic security heightens the stress of parenthood and intensifies relationship problems. One may expect more regressive responses on the part of parents in families where there is economic strain. When regression occurs in the adult, it is not as normal an aspect of the growth process as it is in the adolescent. Because the demands of adult life are likely to be more consistently inescapable than those in adolescence and because the personality is more rigidly formed, retreats to more satisfying life periods of the past may bring a more lasting fixation. Affirming the adult's strengths, helping him to look and plan beyond the overwhelming present, relieving sources of insecurity, pressure and strain so that his burden is more nearly commensurate with his capacity – all these are measures social workers use in order to help the adult in an economic crisis to carry his important task of parenthood more competently. Helping him to look beyond the present to the future is not always a simple task when the present is exerting great pressure. Yet innumerable examples of help of this nature that have been deeply influential in the lives of people could be cited. For example:

Mrs J, the widowed mother of four children who were receiving social security benefits, had grown deeply discouraged and apathetic in the struggle to maintain her family. Her physical complaints (without organic basis), lax housekeeping, impatience, and a general state of unhappiness were affecting the lives of the entire family. Mrs J expressed a feeling of hopelessness; not only did her own life stretch out ahead as an endless path of meagre living and unfulfilled aspirations, but also she felt keenly the poor prospect for her children. What chance had they to do any better? The worker's resourceful suggestion of a scholarship association to enable the intellectually able eldest son to continue his education beyond high school, and his help in putting the mother in touch with music and art classes for two other children, brought a marked change in this woman's morale. Through her children she could now envisage a better future and with them work for its realization.

Sometimes social workers grow discouraged – so many families need so much that the little that can be done hardly seems to matter. Sometimes this is true, yet once again we encounter a surprising element in human nature. With persons in great need a little help may go a long way and prove to be the toehold in a seemingly insurmountable wall.

Some workers tend to be tolerant of parental failure
Among all human limitations, parental shortcomings are often the most difficult for a social worker to accept. To the neglectful, punitive, complaining, begrudging parent who has a meagre capacity to meet his children's needs, the social worker may respond with deep feelings of condemnation. While he may not let these feelings interfere with helping the parent, still he may render the agency's service in such a way as to convey his feelings. Also, in rendering casework services in accordance with the need and request of such parents, he may fail to accord them understanding help and unconsciously may become authoritative or depriving. His identification with the children as opposed to the parents, may lead him to exert demands on their behalf that are beyond the parents' scope. In so doing, he increases the pressure of parental responsibilities and may stimulate in the parent greater neglect or hostility towards the children. This behaviour adaptation, formerly described as regression, occurs when the demands of the external world exceed the individual's capacity to meet those demands. Idealization of their own parents, adherence to the traditional concept of parents as all-giving and all-enduring, together with elements of frustration in their own relationships with their parents, may combine to make workers singularly intolerant of parental failure.

As social workers gradually learn that the parent who fails frequently has been failed, as they comprehend the principle that we give as we are given to and that none of us can give from a vacuum, then they may become more sympathetic with an understanding of the deprived person who deprives, the punished one who punishes. Gradually, then, they may perceive the futility of their own unwittingly retaliative treatment of these parents. It becomes obvious that sympathy, understanding and supportive help may enable these parents to carry their responsibilities more competently, provided their need is not insatiable, as in the case of many people who should be considered emotionally ill. It becomes equally obvious that dislike, condemnation and denial will only undermine further their adequacy as parents.

The focus should not be wholly on the children

In our attempts to help parents with problems of child rearing, we frequently defeat our purpose through focusing wholly on the children and their welfare. In such instances, we may give the parent a feeling that we have little faith in his competence. He may infer that, because he is receiving a child welfare service, we are demanding that he should meet our requirements and are tending to direct the management of his parental responsibilities. Repeatedly, in response to this approach, we see parents become defensive and antagonistic. This might be avoided if the parent had an opportunity to reveal his problems spontaneously in response to our interest in him and to an expressed concern as to how things are going. Our understanding of his experience as a parent will frequently free him to bring out the negative elements in this and enable him to reach out for help if he needs it. Instead, we more often make him defensive about his need for help through immediate routine and meticulous inquiries about the children, their health, their school records, their behaviour and the like. It is commonplace knowledge that in order to help children, we must frequently first help the parents. Often, however, our well-intentioned help has taken the form of coercive measures or persuasive efforts based on our understanding of the child's needs rather than the parent's equally imperative need. When we learn to give to parents in order that they may give to their children, we work more effectively. This principle is particularly significant in our work with families in which the aim of the service is to meet the needs of the child in his own home under the care of his parents or other relatives.

OLD AGE CAN BE A SATISFYING PERIOD

Old age is the last of a series of adaptive changes in the life of the individual. Like other life periods, the person's adaptation to it depends on the general life situation, the extent and suddenness of changes in his circumstances, the nature of previous relationships, and the way in which earlier life crises such as puberty, separation from parents, marriage, parenthood and menopause have been met. Normally, it is a period of diminishing powers in which the individual's inner resources decline, while at the same time his external world narrows, in some instances markedly. *In favourable circumstances of economic security, a gradual decline in physical and mental powers, the continuance of sustaining relationships, the continuance of some satisfying activity, and an inherent capacity on the part of the individual to accept change without undue anxiety and resistance, one may encounter no marked problems of adjustment.* This life period may be one of continued fulfilment, a beneficent twilight period, a reflective and peaceful respite, as glorified by Cicero in 'De Senectute'.

A competitive society tends to make old age difficult

The modern social and economic order operates against this idyllic state in the closing years of life, even when physical health factors are relatively favourable. A competitive society in which the individual's sense of worth has been maintained through achievement and in which people in general have been improvident in the arts of leisure, implies a profound loss of security and of satisfying activity in old age even for many people with advantages. A competitive society has made it impossible for the majority to enjoy economic security and to remain highly valued in the group as they become economically useless and a threat to those who are struggling for a precarious survival. *The old have tended to become a burden rather than an asset in a society in which change has been so rapid that the knowledge and experience of the past have been quickly outmoded and in which productivity oriented to the present and the future is valued more highly than historical perspective or the wisdom of the ages or the affectional contribution in relationship the old can give.*

More often than not, the individual also undergoes a marked physical change, a general lessening of capacity for sustained work, increased fatigability, a general slowing up, often accompanied by chronic and progressive illness of a disabling nature. Loss of physical adequacy, lessened mental adequacy, accompanied by affectional deprivations occasioned through the death of contemporaries and loss of children to other relationships that now become primary for them, loss of gratification in work and in an active social life in the group – all these deprivations and frustrations may combine to give the aged person a deep sense of helplessness. All this may cause a heightened need to depend on others in a life situation in which relationships are less sustaining than before. Frequently old people have a wish to feel adequate and a longing to be needed at a time when reality makes their wishes unrealistic. These are some of the outstanding conflicts of the old; any one of them could well provide anxiety, and a combination of them frequently results in profound anxiety and acute fears. How may old people handle this anxiety?

The old person deals variously with his anxiety
Denial and compensatory activity are common ways of dealing with anxiety. We are all familiar with the old person who denies his failing vision, insisting that he can see just as well as ever, or who denies his loss of physical strength, refusing to be waited on and repudiating the small considerations and social amenities extended to the aged. We are familiar with the compensatory features that may accompany such denials, in which the individual attempts by force to preserve his earlier status. A denial of displacement as head of the family may be accompanied by despotic authority over children and grandchildren. If the authority is not unquestioningly accepted as of old, there may be hysterical episodes or illness. When change is denied, the individual may show deep resentment when any help is offered and may construe it as an attempt at authoritarian management. Sometimes there is a two-way feeling for the person, sensing his growing helplessness, wants on the one hand to give up and become more dependent, while on the other hand he resents his loss of adequacy and wants to maintain it. His protests against management are sometimes a bid for it, and he may quickly and with gratification succumb when circumstances force the issue.

Miss S was growing so infirm as to be unable to care for herself adequately. The social worker tried to help her to face her need for institutional care, only to have the suggestion staunchly repudiated. Finally, eviction by three successive landlords because of neighbours' complaints about the state of her rooms and inability to obtain a fourth lodging led to her going into a home for the aged where she subsequently led a more comfortable and satisfying life. On the day of removal, she angrily reproached the worker for not having 'made her' do this earlier, and at this time she recounted the discomforts and loneliness of the past months.

It is possible that this woman had to live through this last defence against becoming dependent, that she had to experience this final unrealistic assertion of her ability to manage her own life, and that impersonal circumstance alone could serve as an acceptable coercive agent. One wonders, however, whether the social worker who tried to help her to face her need for institutional care might not, without using either coercion or persuasion, have been more helpful than he was. The record shows that the worker focused narrowly and directly on the woman's limitations, pointing out her helplessness, the dangers to her welfare in remaining alone, and stressing the benefits of an old people's home. Had he helped the woman to express her fear of change, her preconceived notions of institutional life, what it meant to part with many of her own things and to give up the management of her own affairs, the woman might have made this choice for herself. We cannot talk people out of their resistance to change, but frequently that resistance may dissipate itself when the individual has an opportunity to give expression to it, especially to a person who understands but does not necessarily feel the same way about it.[1] In this instance the woman might have been spared months of uncomfortable living and much anxiety.

Adaptations are the same as at earlier life periods
In old age the future is uncertain, even frightening, while the present has many frustrations. It is therefore, inevitable that there should be considerable regression to the past. Regressions at this period are normal and absence of them is unusual. Regressions are manifested in many forms varying from individual to individual. Old people frequently attach themselves to old things; they fall back on fixed routines, becoming irritated when forced into unfamiliar regimes. They tend to reminisce about old friends and to idealize the past. They may become untidy or sometimes more meticulous, demanding excessive personal care. They may become blissfully oblivious to present threatening realities, showing an exaggerated optimism and a complete disinclination to plan realistically. Or they may exaggerate present problems, showing marked anxiety about trifling incidents

[1] For a discussion of this concept, see chapter 1, pp. 29–30.

and taking excessive measures to safeguard their health, their finances, and the like. As they experience the reversal of roles in which they feel themselves to be dependent on their children, rather than the children dependent on them, they may ally themselves with young grandchildren and, combating parental authority, may seek indulgence for them. Or they may be rivalrous with the grandchildren. Personality changes may have an organic basis in cerebral damage in the ageing process or may be owing primarily to factors previously enumerated – i.e. to the individual's emotional response, to the many marked changes time brings, sometimes gradually or often quite suddenly. In work with the old, therefore, it is often important to determine the basis of personality change through medical examination. This may guide us in deciding how much to rely on any possible modifications in the environment to bring change in the individual's response.

IMPLICATIONS FOR SOCIAL SERVICES

The decisive point in this life period is that the same behaviour adaptations are being used as at earlier life periods and that the denials of reality, the compensatory efforts, the regressions are serving the same purpose. Now, as formerly, the individual is striving for a feeling of safety and of security. We may do rather different things for the old, our work with them will have a different focus and emphasis, but the same principles are valid.

1. We are interested first in gauging what strengths the person still has to manage his own affairs and helping him to find satisfying activity within the limits of his physical and mental condition and his environmental situation. We try to afford every opportunity for him to utilize these strengths in planning for himself. We give him as much help as we can in relation to what he needs in securing a life situation that makes continued activity possible. Our help may involve utilization of community resources and resources in family relationship.

2. After making sure that the individual has every opportunity to utilize the present to the utmost, so that he is not needlessly driven to the past, we accept some regression to the past as natural, inevitable and essential to his comfort. When we accept this, we may then expect to meet dependency through giving supportive help in many ways, with recognition of the difference between relevant measures at this life period and at earlier ages.

5

DISABILITY AND HANDICAP

All social workers see many individuals who are chronically ill or have a physical disability or handicap. These people present special problems, and therefore workers frequently set them apart as persons who must be treated differently. It is important to bear in mind that, in spite of special problems that demand special services, work with the ill, the disabled and the handicapped is governed by the same basic principles as work with any other group of people.

THE MEANING OF DISABILITY TO THE INDIVIDUAL IS IMPORTANT

It is important, first, to understand the meaning of the illness or handicap to the individual person. His life will be affected both in his circumstances and psychologically in various ways and degrees. In so far as they bring change, the factors determining the nature and degree of the individual's response are age, sex, prior life experience, prior personality development, and the timing of the onset of the disability or handicap in relation to other events in his life. This factor of timing is sometimes decisive. For example, a man immersed in humiliation and defeat at being unemployed may sustain an injury or fall ill. At such a time the disability may be seized on and used to the utmost as a more acceptable basis for being unemployed than not being wanted in the labour market. The same mishap in time of employment might not have brought the same gratifications and therefore, not being useful, would not be clung to in the same way.

In old age, when the future is uncertain and life in general has become frustrating, illness or disability may be used as a means to return to earlier infantile gratifications. The person may gain attention and a feeling of safety and comfort through the care his disability earns him. This is not necessarily so, however, for if the person has well-entrenched patterns of self-dependence, he may resist his disability or deny its existence through refusing medical care and attempting to carry on as before. An important factor determining his choice of a solution may be the response of family members to his disability. Their anxious overprotection may drive him to further lengths in denying his limitations or it may encourage regression. Their indifference and neglect may provoke regression in order to command attention or it may prevent him from getting the help he genuinely needs.

Likewise in adolescence when the young person does not have a secure place in the adult world and has considerable anxiety about his status among his peers, a physical disability, handicap or chronic illness that limits his activity may be deeply disturbing. He may solve the problem by a regression to childhood or may resist the limiting reality of his handicap through overreaching himself in activity and refusing to use measures proffered to safeguard his welfare. Again, decisive factors determining the nature of his response are his prior personality development whether the handicap is congenital or acquired, and the response of others, notably his family and friends, to it. Above all, he may need help in planning realistically for the future.

Illness or handicap may serve a useful purpose

If we understand the meaning of illness or handicap to the individual we may see the purpose it serves for him. Within the framework of his present situation and the interplay of his family relationships, we need to try to understand what *use* his disability has for him – what unmet need it fulfils – now, in his present life situation. Accordingly we ask ourselves such questions as: Why does he not want to give up his disability if it could be cured? Why does he need to deny it? Is it enabling him to escape overwhelming pressures, to compensate for certain lacks, or to gain satisfaction in one way or another? We seek the answer through knowing the individual, focusing on more than his disability; frequently we fail to understand the disabled person because we do not see beyond his disability. Perhaps our own limitations, physical or otherwise, brought us the experience of feeling different, so that as we encounter 'the disabled' it may be difficult not to emphasize his difference and to stress the disablement as though it were the total person rather than merely an aspect of him or as one problem he presents.

The worker in the case of Miss S tended to do this.[1] In attempting to help her to see that an institution would afford her a more comfortable life, he focused on the woman's physical ineptitude, her inability to get along, and thus, perhaps, aroused a strong defence in which Miss S may have been driven to prove that she could and would manage on her own. Had the worker focused on understanding Miss S as a person, he would have helped her express something of what her infirmity meant to her, something of the loneliness and dissatisfactions of her present life as well as her fear of institutions. Thus he might have enabled her to make this choice and thereby to realize constructively her desire to manage her own affairs. Likewise, in the case of Mr D, the worker saw Mr D as a tuberculous patient rather than as a man who had been the head of his family and who still had both the inclination and the capacity for participation in the management of family affairs.[2]

Congenital handicaps may shape the personality

When physical handicap has been congenital or has had its onset in infancy or early childhood, it does not have the same threat of change as when it occurs later in life. It may have had a deep influence, however, in forming the personality of the individual. The effect it has had in these instances will depend largely on the meaning the handicap has had for parents and other family members responsible for the care of the individual during childhood. Frequently, a parent brings to the experience of having a child certain predetermined needs that may lead him to seek self-realization, or sometimes even to strive for adjustment, through the child. When the child is born handicapped or early on suffers a handicapping condition or chronic illness, the parent may experience great personal frustration. It may also be a threat to his pride, thus making him feel inferior. The resultant feelings of irritation, especially if he feels at all to blame for the child's condition, may lead to feelings of rejection. This rejection may be expressed openly or, if the parent feels guilty over his hostile feelings, may be disguised through overprotective handling that eases the guilt.

If the parent has had deep feelings of inadequacy or great frustrations, he may identify himself closely with a handicapped child, and in such an instance protective handling or unrealistic, wishful strivings may characterize his relationship with the child.

[1] See chapter 4, pp. 92–93.
[2] See chapter 2, pp. 32–33.

G

In such a family Mr V, unemployed because of a serious cardiac condition, had cut short an able career in the engineering field. He responded to his son's post-polio handicap and mental retardation with refusal to accept a clinic's advice regarding medical care and vocational training. He needed to deny that there was anything much wrong with the boy. He blamed the school for the boy's failure and resisted placing him in a school for crippled children where it was thought the youngster would have a better chance for some success.

As workers confer with parents on problems presented by their handicapped children it is important that they should understand what the child and his handicap mean to the parent. This understanding can serve as a guide in our efforts to help parents who turn to us not only in relation to management of their children but also in such vital decisions as to whether the children should have special education in a day or residential school, or co-operate in medical care.

Understanding an adult's response may enable the worker to be more helpful
When we work with the adult whose handicap has been lifelong, it will be too late to bring about basic personality change. Understanding his response may, however, enable us to be more helpful in many ways. For example:

Mr and Mrs N were a young couple who were both blind. They were living in basement rooms in a dilapidated building. Mr and Mrs N had met in a home for the blind and had been married shortly after leaving there while both were employed in a blind and handicapped persons' workshop. Mrs N, aged twenty, received social security and other services when she became pregnant and could no longer work. When his wife was unable to accompany him back and forth from the shop and in their rounds Mr N gave up his work, maintaining that he could not get along without her. During the subsequent months he became increasingly dependent on her. After the birth of a child with normal sight he became irritable and difficult, since the mother became quite absorbed in this fulfilment of her fondest hopes.

It was at this point that Mrs N unburdened to the worker her **great** discouragement over Mr N's inability to assume the responsibilities of a husband and father. She described him as always having been childish, which she attributed to the fact that he lost his parents during infancy and was left to the care of a grandmother who gave him excessive care because of his blindness. Upon marriage he immediately looked to her to plan for both of them. She contrasted her own situation with his in that she had come from a family in which there was hereditary blindness, five of eight members having been sightless or having had markedly impaired vision. She said that her blindness had been taken for granted. Her family was sociable and of great solidarity. The children accepted responsibility and participated almost normally in the life of the community. Mrs N impressed the worker as being an outgoing, sociable woman with unusual self-dependence in managing her affairs and in caring for her child.

As Mrs N spoke of her concern over her husband the worker helped her to consider what the child meant to him, and she was able to identify his difficulty as one of rivalry, although at the time this did not help her to feel any more tolerant of his limitations. The worker's suggestion that she should place more responsibility on him did not bring results. Later the worker tried to get acquainted with Mr N, who had until this time remained almost unknown. The worker found him very unhappy because he was not working and earning, but he disliked his work. He claimed to be mechanically inclined and said that he enjoyed working on old radios. He recalled his life in the home for the blind with some pleasure, especially as he talked of having studied the violin, played in the orchestra and participated in musical activities at a church. In this community he had missed his religious and musical activities and had wanted work of a different sort but had felt that he would not be considered for anything. He was discouraged and depressed about their physical surroundings, and the worker got the impression that their living arrangements had operated against community contacts. The worker agreed that there might be difficulty in finding a job but, in view of the labour shortage and the fact that some industries were now employing blind workers, held out hope that he might get work. He made suggestions as to where Mr N might apply. He showed interest in his musical ability also and in the possibility that he and his wife might find community activities and church connections similar to those they had enjoyed in the past.

Later Mr N obtained work, and shortly thereafter the worker helped him apply for better housing.

Some months later the worker learned from Mrs N that Mr N had continued to be fairly regularly employed, that they hoped the child would be admitted to a nursery school group, and that they had joined a group of young married couples who lived on the housing estate and gave parties. Both Mr and Mrs N were playing in the orchestra for the group's dances. In their last conversation Mrs N stated that her husband had become tolerant of the baby; that he had bought him an electric train for Christmas and, since the baby was too young to enjoy this toy, Mr N was playing with it a great deal. She complained that he had spent a considerable sum of money on a watch, which was foolish in that he could not use it. The worker helped her to see that this possession meant to him 'being like other men'. Mrs N reported general improvement in their relationship, their only present difficulty being over the spending of money. She recounted that their worst quarrel had occurred over some curtains – Mrs N wanted pink ones, while Mr N wanted blue!

INFLUENCE ON THE USE OF SOCIAL SERVICES

This case affords discussion of a number of important points in work with the handicapped:

1. Basic personality differences in Mr and Mrs N result in part from their differing life experience with the same handicap. It is clear that each has different needs in adulthood. There can be no great change in the personality of Mr N but, in so far as his needs are met, he functions more adequately within the limits of his personality.

2. Mr N was apparently ignored. This became a disturbing factor in his relationship with his wife. The worker's eventual recognition of him as a person important in the family scheme apparently brought a ready response. Perhaps because of his handicap and also because of his dependency he needed this recognition all the more.

3. We note also that marked change had come into the lives of Mr and Mrs N through transferring from the protected regime of an institution, where they lived among the handicapped, to a competitive community in which they must find their place among those who are not handicapped. This adjustment was probably more difficult for Mr N because he was basically a more dependent

person than his wife. He had clung to her to support him within the community, so that when she withdrew from work he had to accompany her. He needed encouragement and supportive help from someone who represented the community. It might be expected that in work with blind individuals who have lived in an institution there would frequently be a need for help in using community resources and in finding some of the interests of their past life in the strange situation.

4. This case also emphasizes the significant fact that 'the blind' are not necessarily helpless, and that in spite of, or perhaps all the more because of, their difference from others, they long for association with those who have normal vision. They try to see the world through our eyes to a greater extent perhaps than we try to see it through theirs. Watches and colours and respectable surroundings still matter. All Mr N's needs were needs frequently encountered in work with sighted fathers and husbands. The blind individual is a *person* who happens to be blind. We need to know the person in order to help with the problem of blindness. This same principle applies with handicaps other than blindness.

5. Correspondence with the school attended by Mr N revealed that there had been no attempt to determine his intellectual capacity, vocational aptitudes, or aspirations and interests. It is obvious that persons with a major handicap need special help and special opportunities that may enable them to overcome their limitations as much as possible. Dependence, actual and psychological, is an inevitable result of a lack of preparation for the life of the community. When the person's prior life experience has been such as to induce dependency, he may have all the more need for this help. We note the importance also of using all available community resources both for preventive and remedial medical care.

The worker's feelings about handicaps are important
In our work with disabled and handicapped people, traditional attitudes – certain time-honoured emphases – frequently obstruct us, perhaps because we feel deeply about them. We encounter our own mixed feelings about persons who are different. In many of us there probably are vestiges of our early childhood anxiety about difference. In any group of children we can note anxiety about the child who is a stranger until the group has felt him out and been assured of his likeness to them. We have all observed their reactions to the child who is markedly different – in dress, in ways or in

language. A handicapped child frequently becomes the target of much hostility. Often they cannot permit themselves to identify with him. Perhaps this is because of an unconscious fear that whatever happened to him might happen to them. Therefore, they may ostracize him in one way or another as a protection against entering into a relationship that is somehow threatening. As they grow older, parental disapproval may check this savagery. Also, as they mature they become more altruistic, and guilt over past feelings towards or treatment of those who are less fortunate may bring a reversal of attitudes and behaviour.

Adult attitudes towards handicapped people are characterized by an inability to take handicaps for granted, by overprotective tendencies, and by a degree and kind of emotional involvement that tends to set the person apart. These feelings are reflected in disability-conscious efforts to help them. Perhaps these feelings explain our studied attitudes, our concentration on just *how to treat* the handicapped – as though they were a separate species. This is shown in our tendency to see these individuals in terms of their handicap and to plan for them primarily with reference to their difference, thereby frequently enhancing their discomfort and feeling of isolation.

Feelings as a person must be understood
Much work with the handicapped has been done with the self-conscious conviction that certain attitudes should be maintained by individuals who work with them. We have been aware that some handicapped people have tended to become dependent. The prominence of regressive impulses in response to the obstacles or the change incurred in the individual's life led to an emphasis on not infantilizing the handicapped. Workers have been cautioned to avoid sympathizing with them and to encourage a certain bravado through reassuring them and 'bucking them up'. In accordance with this, some workers have avoided discussing the handicap lest the individual should become too centred on his handicap. A number of such attitudes could be cited that show our studied efforts to help those *we feel* are different. Our helping efforts have swung from the extreme of coddling and sympathy that weaken, to the discipline and denial that also may not strengthen. The decisive point is that these stock attitudes are not valid for general use. They meet the needs of some individuals but frustrate others. We will help the handicapped individual only as we understand his *needs as a person*,

not only the needs created by his handicap but also those he has in common with other human beings. This focus implies readiness to acknowledge his difficulties, help him express his feelings about them, offer protective measures and supportive help in accordance with his need, and let him use his strengths and resourcefulness in managing his own affairs to whatever extent is possible. The same principles we use in helping people with other problems are appropriate in work with those who are chronically ill or physically handicapped.

6

THE FAMILY

We have considered some of the common needs of people as individuals at different stages of life and as individuals participating in the group, family and community. The importance of family life to the child as preparation for life in the world and for the part he will play in the establishment and maintenance of another family has been suggested although not depicted comprehensively. The interplay of relationships within a family is normally complex and to discuss the various anomalies in human adjustment that relate to the organization of the family and to the varying nature of its interrelationships is beyond the limits of this presentation.

Conflicts may be heightened in families receiving social services
Since social workers deal with families at times when bewildering complications try them, families who have frequently known repeated crises or shocks, the normal struggle of each family member for closeness to the family and for apartness from it can well be heightened. *The conflicts are essentially the same, only perhaps more intense, with a greater emotional stake in decisions that involve dependency or separation.*

(i) Mr J, who grew up in a family where he was the mother's dependent son, has had a difficult time maintaining his place in the world apart from his parents by supporting his wife and children. Now, in receiving a social service on account of illness, his parents are also significant. While he knows that with some sacrifice they not only could help him but would willingly do so, his very survival as an adequate adult male is at stake in his protest against turning to them or their knowing of his predicament. Even his illness does not justify or ease the situation. His marriage is threatened, for again, as in its early days, his mother will hold the ascendant position and the struggle to place his wife first, which he had practically won, could well be lost in the return to dependence on his parents.

(ii) Miss C had clung to her family in spite of early impulses to break away. Throughout her childhood and adolescence she had been outdone by a sister whom she felt her parents greatly preferred. Her resentment bade her break off and find a life of her own, but guilt over this same resentment, together with a persistent need to be needed, forbade the going. This seemingly curious reaction of staying because one wants to go is not uncommon. A normal separation would have been an enactment of her rejection, so she stayed, contributing to the support of the family group for many years. Finally, the 'life of her own' came about through the death of the mother, when the father went to live with the 'preferred' sister. Later, when this sister was feeling the strain the worker found in Miss C a woman who unquestionably could help, but who offered many reasons for being unable to do so and who finally, under pressure, strongly asserted her right to a life of her own. Perhaps she had an unconscious need to withhold love as she felt the father had withheld love from her, expressed in her words to the effect that her sister could take care of him, he always liked her, he chose to go to live with her, and so on.

(iii) Mr O, a successful engineer, was earning good money. His wife also was earning and yet, when approached to help his aged father, he gave many reasons for being absolutely unable to give his father a home or to contribute to his support elsewhere. The real reason lay in this man's long-standing resentment towards his father who, in his opinion, 'let me and my sister down' following their mother's death, when he married another woman. 'Let *her* children look after him' was his attitude, since it was their mother who enjoyed the most productive years of the father's life and spent his money.

Understanding family life gives new meaning to the responsibility of relatives
As the carry-over of the family conflicts about dependence versus separation in later life is viewed in relation to attitudes towards

responsibility for family members, one might, at the risk of over-simplification, make the following tentative statements:

1. In general, when an individual has had satisfying and constructive love relationships within the family, he attains the capacity to meet the dependence of family members. In such relationships, the impulse is to share and to take responsibility if it is possible to do so.

2. Frequently, when the individual is still tied to the family but has much resentment over those ties, plus a fear of loss of love and anxiety over guilt if he should not fulfil his obligation, the problem is that of the relative himself who is unrealistic about his ability to take responsibility. He may share his last crust and mortgage his own future because he is not emotionally free to say, 'I am not able to help.' To refuse would be to enact his feelings of rejection and also to risk loss of relationships in which he still has a certain childish dependence.

3. In general, when the individual's separation from the family has not been a normal process of emancipation but a cutting off or breaking away in order to survive, involvement in the family through a renewal of dependency or through contributing to its support constitutes a painful reopening of old wounds or a threatening entanglement in an old frustrating net. In such an instance the person may unrealistically refuse help or maintain his inability to help, building up a strong case for himself. Sometimes, in order to survive as a relatively free person with some chance for growth, he cannot permit himself to become entangled in his past.

In summary, then, we might say that when relationships are sufficiently good to make acceptance of responsibility for others a constructive experience, the individual will be inclined to assume this responsibility if he is able to do so.

Adversity need not undermine family life

While recognizing that conflicts in families where there is poverty may be heightened through the anxieties and uncertainties implicit in their circumstances, we must *not* assume that this is always true or that these families inevitably abound in problematic relationships that obstruct normal development of the children. Sometimes these very stresses seem to have made relationships more constructive. Social workers know that in the families of the poor one may find solidarity, a willingness to share, to live beyond narrow absorption in self for others, on the part of both parents and children. It has sometimes seemed that because they have so little else, family ties have been enhanced and used to the utmost in the realization of growth. The fortitude, the resilience, the capacity for resourceful planning – in short, all the many strengths that arouse our wonder and our respect – show good basic relationships. Whether these have endured in spite of adversity or whether they are in part its product is difficult to say. A long tradition exalts the benefits of poverty. It has always been an easy way out as well as a comfortable philosophy for the 'haves' in relation to the 'have-nots'.

Traditional attitudes, however, frequently stem from wishful thinking as an escape from the solution of difficult problems or to ease our social conscience. On the basis of his findings, the modern student of human behaviour and social conditions departs from traditional attitudes towards adverse circumstance. He concludes that, while poverty may not necessarily undermine family life, it greatly endangers it and makes the individual's survival as a social-ized person a more precarious struggle and one with a more dubious outcome. He knows that in more advantageous circumstances the strengths frequently manifested among the disadvantaged might be reinforced and utilized beyond self-survival. In his eyes, man's fortitude and resilience under adversity constitute a strong argument for greater opportunity.

Social services should strengthen family life
Social services should be administered so as to strengthen family life in the interests of the individual and society. What the service is doing to the life of the family should be uppermost in the minds of each staff member.

THE INTERPLAY OF FAMILY RELATIONSHIPS

Understanding what is happening to family life implies some knowledge of what it has been, some perception of its strengths and weaknesses. This involves learning something of how the family functioned as a group prior to the present difficulty. Just as the individual commonly has varying needs at different age levels and common ways of responding in so far as these needs are met or not met, just as these needs and ways of reacting must be respected if the individual is to be helped, so the family group presents a varied interplay of relationship needs that must be considered if its strengths are to be conserved and disintegration guarded against. Further-more, we often encounter the family at times of marked change.

The difficulties that bring a family to social agencies may have set in operation a realignment of the roles played by individuals within the group.

Workers enter the scene at a time of instability
Social workers enter the family scene at a time of instability when the life of the group is reshaping itself or is being refashioned by circumstance. Our service and the way it is rendered, as a new and foreign element in a changing scene, may play a decisive part in the family's future. It is well for workers to have some awareness of the part they play in order (*a*) not to interfere unwittingly either with the formation of new interfamily patterns or with the old inter-relationships, which still serve a purpose, and (*b*) to lend themselves to constructive rather than destructive use in the interplay of the group.

In the D family we encountered a group in which the father, the head of the household in more than a nominal sense, had seemingly been withdrawn from participation in family life through illness.[1] Understanding of his old position in the home and of the mother's unreadiness to assume his role, together with information on his present health condition and attitudes towards his family responsibilities, might have enabled the worker to be more helpful about the medical plan suggested by the physician for the welfare of the group. This would have implied recognition and utilization of the father's established patterns as head of the household in planning for himself. In the case of John P, the family was first seen at a time of change when the boy's new adult status as wage earner brought him into a new relationship with his parents, one so full of problems that he had to solve it through withdrawal from the group.[2] Some understanding of the significance of the family interplay might have saved the worker futile efforts and enabled him to be more helpful to the mother in her search for help in coping with a recalcitrant son.

Workers must understand family patterns and their implications
It is important that workers should be encouraged to observe and try to understand the interplay of relationships within the family. This implies some knowledge of common family patterns and awareness of the significant indicators of the nature of the relation-

[1] See chapter 2, pp. 32–33.
[2] See chapter 3, pp. 76–78.

ships and their meaning to the individuals concerned. Roughly speaking, these family patterns might be grouped as: (*a*) family responsibilities shared by both parents, (*b*) father the head of the household and the dominant member, (*c*) mother the head of the household and the dominant member, (*d*) family responsibilities evaded by both parents. With great oversimplification, some of the implications of these types of family organization for children might be described as follows:

1. The family in which parental responsibilities have been or are carried jointly and in which there seems to have been mutual sharing in many aspects of life, such as financial management, companionship with children, discipline of children, recreation opportunities, religious activity and the like, theoretically shows the pattern most favourable to the child's development. Such a sharing is generally conducive to a harmonious home atmosphere, security in relationship with both parents, a minimum of hostile rivalry between brothers and sisters, and a minimum of conflict in growing up. In most families, certain individuals will be found in close identification with one another; these identifications will normally shift from time to time, frequently in accordance with the age of the child and with his growth needs at a particular period. For example, Johnny may be clearly seen as a 'father's boy'. It is not merely that he looks and acts like him; there is a bond of feeling between the two that defies analysis but which is a discernible 'feeling together' about all things and towards all the others in the group. Of several sons, Johnny is 'the apple of his father's eye' and the father is the pivot of Johnny's world. These alignments, which occur normally in all families, may be less well defined and less fixed in the family in which both parents have a real place through joint sharing of family life. Certainly, although they are present they may escape becoming the focal points of controversy, of rivalry and of antagonism as in some other families.

In social services, we often encounter these families when the joint relationship of the parents is thrown out of balance temporarily or permanently. The inability of one parent or the other to function normally – perhaps because of unemployment, illness or handicap, or the loss of one parent from the group – will bring some change throughout all the relationships in the group. In many instances, a relationship of mutual sharing between parents may have been dislocated through the addition to the family of an aged grandparent. The significant factor to observe is how the remaining parent, or the parent with a changed status, is adapting to his or her new part and how others are responding to the change. Is a widowed mother taking over formerly shared responsibilities readily, with great uncertainty, or with a marked protest against her fate? Is the wife of a now handicapped man assuming her heavier load with irritation, with some gratification, with hostility towards or understanding of her husband's predicament, with some acceptance or with complete rejection of the adverse circumstance in her life? Is the place of a woman whose aged mother-in-law now lives in the home being usurped? And if so, how is she responding to the situation and what reverberations are being registered throughout the group? Because a relationship that has been one of joint sharing has often been based on the relatively mature development of each individual, one frequently finds resourceful adaptation to the imposed change with a minimum of threat to the solidarity of the family group. Change may be causing discomfort or stress, but the essential strengths of the relationship still make possible a constructive adaptation of one sort or another. These families present fewer problems in their use of services than some other families, but even so there are advantages in the worker's recognition of the needs they present and the strengths that are here to be maintained and utilized. The G family seemingly typifies such a situation.[1]

2. A second pattern appears in the family in which the father carries the major responsibility and occupies first place in the affairs of the family. He not only brings in the money but also decides how it shall be spent. He dictates the management of the children, assumes the major disciplinary role, and fashions the family's recreational life, educational plans and religious practice primarily in accordance with his own taste and inclination. Whether or not the family life is essentially harmonious will depend on many variable factors, such as how hostile or beneficent a head the father is, how rigid his need is to play the dominating part or the extent to which he can modify it in accordance with the needs of others, and what his dominating ways mean to the mother. If her dependency needs are met in ways that are gratifying, there may be little parental conflict and the children at least have the security afforded through a vested authority in the home. If the mother is deeply frustrated and only outwardly submissive, her irritations may be expressed

[1] See chapter 2, pp. 48–50.

in devious ways and the children may live in a tense atmosphere and be surrounded by a parental conflict in which they become the pawns.

This family pattern is more usual in some cultures than in others, but from the standpoint of modern psychology – regardless of the culture factor – this family structure is theoretically not altogether favourable for preparing the child for life in contemporary society. Whether or not the home is harmonious, there will be less security in relationships with both parents and greater variation in values for the several children within the family. Those children, especially the boys who happen to identify themselves with the father, may have a secure status, but more often than not in the process of growing up they may come into acute conflict with his authority. There is a great chance for the development of deep dependencies, for the formation of hostile rivalries between brothers and sisters, and for the development of a sense of inadequacy on the part of all the children as they measure themselves against the father – particularly on the part of those who are close to the dominated mother. The alignments in such a family will tend to be well defined and sometimes they are rigid, i.e. permanently fixed. They tend also to become the focal points of rivalries and antagonisms, and the family is frequently divided into two camps, one against the other. This is likely to be true when the mother has been in conflict over her place in the relationship.

These families are often encountered at a time when this parental relationship also is thrown out of balance. It might be thought that the change would inevitably be for the better, but this is not necessarily so; in fact, the members of such a family may have a difficult time not only in meeting adverse circumstances but also in their relationships with one another. Again the significant factor to observe is how the remaining parent or the parent with a changed status is adapting to his or her new part and how others are responding to the change that has occurred. For example, is the widowed mother quite lost and confused because of the necessity to assume a leadership role? Does she instead show considerable gratification in her freedom though with some resultant anxiety that leads her to idealize her husband and dramatize her loss? Is the wife of a now handicapped man unable to assume more responsibility than formerly and afraid of taking any initiative because it seems like a gesture of hostility against him? This was the plight of Mrs D, who could only say, 'I cannot put him out of the house,' and 'What would the neighbours think?'.[1] Does the suddenly dethroned man cling to his former status or does he regress into infantile dependency, asserting his will in a new way? Are the children, with the sudden loss of an authoritative hand, in open revolt against a father who has lost his power or oblivious of the controls set by an ineffectual mother? Because a relationship in which the outstanding characteristic has been an unequal distribution of authority and dependency has often had as its base the relatively immature development of one or both parents, we frequently find that the imposed change is causing a reaction of considerable anxiety and some breakdown of what formerly seemed to be family solidarity. Actually, these families sometimes typify the house that is divided against itself, so that when adversity comes its schisms are widened and the relationships are maintained with great difficulty. These families may present many problems in their use of services, and it is important that the worker should recognize the need for supportive help at certain points in a period of adjustment to change that is fraught with deeply disturbing emotional conflicts for the individuals concerned.

3. A third pattern is that of the family in which the mother carries the major responsibility and occupies first place in the affairs of the family. She manages the money and carries the burden of planning for and managing the children. It is her ambition and her efforts that keep things going, with or without the co-operation of a father who may be passive and dependent or ineffectually protesting and dependent. Social workers have encountered many such families and have learned the importance of knowing whether the woman is playing the dominant part out of a deep need to dominate the man or because this role has been forced on her through circumstance. Some women with a capacity and a desire to share responsibility have been forced into carrying the major burden by their concern for the welfare of the children. This has occurred in instances when the husband has been deeply dependent and ineffectual or has been rendered ineffectual and demoralized through circumstances outside his control.

Many relatively mature women who have no marked need for dominance fall readily into the part of providing for and protecting their families. They may easily assume a maternal role towards the father if he is basically helpless or rendered so through circumstances. The primacy of the maternal impulse makes them vul-

---

[1] See chapter 2, pp. 32–33.

nerable to this part, to an extent that may undermine the husband's adequacy and have destructive consequences for the children. Sometimes, however, when the husband has a deep dependency this response is not only gratifying but also sustaining and may help him to carry on after a fashion. It has also been commonly observed that the man gains his sense of adequacy and feeling of status in so far as he is able to cope with the world. He measures himself as a man by what he attains as provider for his family. When he meets defeat outside the home, he suffers not merely loss of status there but may not bring much to the role of husband and father. Instead, discouraged and defeated, he may become dependent and look to his wife not only to comfort and reassure him but also to take the leadership in the home.

Social workers encounter many fathers who have been defeated, often through force of circumstance and not necessarily through basic inadequacy. As a result, many mothers are found in a role of dominance that may or may not be wholly gratifying to them but which they are striving to carry for the sake of their families. In these instances the family life may or may not be harmonious. When the mother wants the major responsibility and the husband is satisfied in his dependency, there may be a certain serenity and solidarity in the situation. When the husband's dependency is imposed from without and when the woman is carrying the major responsibility against her inclination, there may be many conflicts for both parents and for the children. As problems arise that bring these families to social agencies, the significant factor to observe is, again, how the remaining parent, or the parent with changed status, is adapting to his or her new part and how others are responding to the change. Is the social problem reinforcing the family pattern through giving the mother an even greater place than she formerly held and through further undermining the father? If so, is the reaction one of gratification or discomfort? In cases when there is discomfort, both parties may be receptive to assistance that strengthens the husband's position, such as employment opportunities or greater participation with the agency in planning for the family.

Whether or not this parental relationship is harmonious, it theoretically presents certain problems for the development of children. While they may receive the protective care during infancy and early childhood essential for basic security in life, they may experience deprivation, insecurity, and feelings of inadequacy in their relationship with the father. The importance of the father relationship in the life of a child, as affording a medium that enables him to move away from dependency on the mother and to find his place in the world outside the home, is well recognized. Some children have a problem in growing up, either because the father is basically dependent or because he has been forced into dependency through finding the world too much for him. Alignments in these families, particularly when there is parental conflict and discomfort, are well defined, and again one may find a house divided against itself, in that the children are strongly aligned with the mother against the father, who is a rival for her affections, or some of them may be identified defensively with the inadequate father while the others take on the strong mother's more aggressive patterns. These alignments, again, may become the focal points on which rivalries and antagonisms are centred. These families may present many problems. One frequently noted is the tendency of the mother to carry undue responsibility for the family in handling its affairs with a social agency. Unless she has an inherent need to subordinate the father, she may welcome opportunities to include him in plans. Furthermore, he may be receptive to recognition, so that his active involvement may prove to be a step towards rehabilitation.

4. In still another family pattern, neither parent wants or assumes a responsible role and each resists being head of the family. Each charges the other with irresponsibility or laxity and each nags the other to take more responsibility. 'They are your children too,' may be an oft-reiterated charge. Theoretically, this is the least favourable configuration for the development of children. Home life is frankly discordant and there is marked insecurity in relationships with both parents. This situation creates a maximum of hostile rivalry among brothers and sisters, who compete anxiously for the fragments of care they can elicit from either or both parents. The alignments within the family may be weak and wavering, for the children shift from one parent to the other in an endless quest for security.

These families are encountered in social agencies when the relationships between the parents has often been rendered even more precarious than formerly. Again, however, it is important to observe how the remaining parent, or the parent with changed status, is adapting to the new situation. These families present many problems as they use social services. Some parents have few strengths and are likely to relegate to the agency as many of their parental responsibilities as a willing worker interested in the welfare of the children will take over. Understanding what they want, need and can use is important for effective service, and these cases often present the problem of protective measures on behalf of the children.

Every aspect of family life reflects family relationships
Since it is important that social workers should understand family interplay in order to safeguard the welfare of the family in the interests of the individual and society, it might be asked how we may achieve this understanding if it is not within our province to explore marital relationships and family interrelationships. *The nature of these relationships is reflected in every aspect of family life.* Everything that is revealed sheds light on the family patterns. If the worker knows something of common family patterns and their significance for his work, the information necessary for a given service will form the groundwork for an understanding of the family as a whole. As the contact continues, this understanding will be supplemented gradually and naturally without infringement of the client's rights if the worker's efforts to understand stem from a genuine interest in the individual.

Recognition of the importance of certain insights into family life should influence favourably not only the worker's inquiry into the family situation but also his use of agency procedures and practices. For example, when he recognizes the importance of learning the place held by the father in a family, he will appreciate the changes that are often imposed on him through illness and unemployment. Seeing this, the worker may alter his current relationship with the family.

When a worker not only knows the relationship needs of the infant and young child but also sees in the specific case the meaning parenthood has for each parent concerned, he may be more helpful to the woman who turns to him for advice as she struggles with the question of whether she should work. When the worker knows something of family relationships, he gives parents who seek his help in difficulties with an aged grandparent sound counsel based not only on his understanding of the needs of the aged but also on his understanding of what this particular person means to the family group as a whole. When administrators know something of the significance of relationships within a family, policies will reflect this understanding.

Respect for family life may change policies and laws
It has been possible to present only sketchily a few common examples of interplay in family life and to suggest briefly how recognition of significant meanings may be used in our work. Perhaps this may stimulate us to draw on our past observations and experience, to look inquiringly into the meanings of the responses between individuals we are encountering in our present experience, and to read more to gain further insight into family life. In all aspects of our work in which we try to help people through social services, we encounter many reflections and vestiges of family life. The child in man is there, modified but at moments amazingly intact, the past urgently active in the present. These needs must be taken into account if we are to help people to maintain their adulthood. The ways of growth and the present family relationship deserve our consideration, both at the administrative level where policies are formulated, and in the day-to-day contacts of the worker with clients. It must be recognized, however, that unsound administrative practices based on unsound or inadequate policies cannot be remedied adequately through casework skills.

PART THREE

SUPERVISION

7

SOME GENERAL PRINCIPLES IN THE LIGHT
OF HUMAN NEEDS AND BEHAVIOUR

Insight into basic motivations in human behaviour and common
human needs is an important aspect of staff development.

Supervision in public social services is an administrative process
that contributes to staff development. Every staff member in a position of responsibility for the work of other staff members has an
obligation to *develop the abilities of the staff* under his immediate
direction in the useful application of knowledge and skills on the
job. This is as a teaching-learning situation, i.e. as an educational
rather than a purely administrative process.

ATTITUDES OF THE WORKER

There is a need in the social services for workers who have considerable capacity to live beyond absorption in self and who are
inclined towards creative activity.[1] To be sure, here, as in other
fields, one may encounter individuals who are conspicuously
unready for professional development. There may be workers whose
excessive need still to be given to compels them to choose and
pursue work with people for purposes of self-gratification. They
may need to be served by the people whom presumably they are
there to serve, and they may use the client as an outlet for their
hostile impulses or frustrated wishes. By and large, however, it is
probable that many workers choose this field of activity because
of their readiness to live beyond themselves, their liking and concern for people as individuals, and their impulse to participate in
and to contribute to the life of the community. If this is so, we can
assume considerable readiness to learn and considerable stamina to
resist regression when the demands of the job are not nicely timed
to the worker's acquisition of knowledge and skill.[2] This assumption

[1] For the relevance of this in the growth process, see chapter 2, pp. 56–58.
[2] For elaboration of the concept of regression, see chapter 2, pp. 54–56.

does not imply an absence of personal need to be realized in their work, but instead readiness to understand and some capacity to deal with such need. The supervisor's understanding of behaviour, motives and principles of personality growth may throw light on the worker's learning response and thus enable him to convey knowledge and impart skills more competently.

Emotions influence use of supervision and learning responses

Since emotions largely dominate our thinking and action, it is important to recognize that workers have strong feelings in helping people and that these feelings will influence what they think and do.[1] Feelings will also operate significantly in the worker's use of supervision and in his learning response. The important part played by the worker's feelings and emotional convictions has been suggested repeatedly throughout this discussion. First, in helping people in time of trouble, the social worker encounters them when they are disturbed, sometimes when they are their least rational selves. In so far as he feels *with* them, which he must do to relate himself to them sympathetically and with understanding, he runs the risk of coming to feel *like* them. It is unfortunate when this occurs, for when we feel the same way about a person's problem as he feels, we cannot help him to cope with it. Instead, our emotional response may reinforce his, thus adding to his confusion and ineptitude. Secondly, the social worker has an ever-varying array of so-called 'lay attitudes' – the deep convictions, prejudices and biases to which every human is heir in his thinking about social problems, human behaviour and the social order, particularly about economic and racial groupings. As he actually encounters certain social problems, he may be deeply moved; as he comes up against behaviour that violates his personal standards, he may be shocked or afraid; as he derives knowledge and gains experience, some of his deepest and most cherished convictions may be challenged. Thus, day in and day out, he is subject to considerable emotional wear and tear. Thirdly, he works within the framework of an agency that is accountable to a community of persons who likewise have pronounced convictions and cherished feelings about different kinds of people in need. He is subject to the pressure of these attitudes, often literally subject to them, for they are imbedded in the law and in agency policies that so govern his activity that he may fail to be critical of them. Alternatively, in blind frustration he may fail to use

[1] See chapter 2, pp. 45–46.

these policies and regulations intelligently or resourcefully, or to work within them productively.

'Lay attitudes' manifest in social work

A few of the 'lay attitudes' commonly brought into social work that may influence the worker's way of extending help are the following.

A conviction that people do not want to work sometimes causes workers to distrust the clients' statements regarding unemployment and his efforts to find employment. The possible demoralizing effect of this on a client seems obvious.

Closely related to this idea is the belief that if one meets dependency freely or economic need adequately, the person will be demoralised. If irresponsibility is more prevalent among the poor than other groups, it can well be a product of too much rather than too little of harsh circumstances. Adult responsibility is always escapable if one basically needs to escape it, i.e. if one has not the strength to assume it. We may also overlook the now well-recognized psychological fact that, in the last analysis, those of us who readily assume the responsibilities of adulthood have been enabled to do so largely through a total experience in which our emotional needs have been met freely while our circumstances have been sufficiently advantageous to give us something to give in relationships with others. Workers who give begrudgingly may undermine rather than strengthen the client's capacities for personality growth. Many workers have been reared in sufficiently comfortable economic circumstances to enable them to accept unquestioningly the idea cherished by their thrifty parents that a man who is 'worthwhile', i.e. thrifty, stable and responsible, will somehow save money for 'a rainy day' regardless of the size of his family or the meagreness of his income. This belief may lead them to minimize strengths in the applicant and to treat him in general as a much less responsible, ambitious and self-respecting person that he is.[1]

Prejudiced attitudes on the part of workers may be encountered in any and all aspects of life. Only a few can be cited to illustrate how they may dominate our work. Workers may think that certain racial or national groups are innately inferior intellectually and morally to other groups. This may lead them to accept unquestioningly a lower standard of living for these people and to withhold needed and desired help with problems, on the assumption that these problems are inherent and that the individuals concerned would

[1] See chapter 2, pp. 42–45.

not make productive use of help. Or considering these people inadequate and less well-endowed to assume responsibility, the worker may take over the management of their affairs in ways that constitute an infringement of their rights.

Workers may have strong feelings about certain human relationships, such as that all mothers should love their children and that it is abnormal or immoral when they do not love them. In such an instance, a worker with these feelings may decide that these parents should be made to assume responsibility for their children. When a mother's desire to work seems to stem from a wish to escape from her children, a worker may make her feel obliged to continue to stay rather than permit her freedom of choice as she weighs up the pros and cons. Or the worker may express disapproval through coercive attitudes in various other ways.[1] On the other hand, financial independence may be so enthroned in the workers' thinking that a mother's desire to remain with her children is discouraged.

Attitudes change with new experiences

What of the attitudes that limit the worker's ability to help the client in terms of his need and that drive him to meet his own needs rather than the client's? Are these attitudes subject to change and can workers be helped to think and feel differently about people? May they gain some awareness of their own feelings so that the client is treated as an individual in his own right rather than as an extension of the worker's self? It is probable that many of these prejudices will *gradually* change as the worker's experience widens. They may change also as the worker encounters new ideas and thinking about social problems in his professional relationships with colleagues as well as through reading. Reading is productive when it is done with the purpose of learning. It is unfortunate that workers sometimes read from fear of others who know more; it may not be helpful if it serves primarily as a defence against one's colleagues who value reading. In so far as prejudices stem from ignorance, misinformation and lack of experience or a narrow one-sided experience, they will give way as new knowledge is attained and as the worker's range of identifications with people widens. Until we know the poor, the rich, the black, the white, the Jew, the Gentile, the Pole, the Greek, the Norwegian, and so on, we may set any one of these groups apart and react to them in terms of misconceptions based on inadequate knowledge and inexperience.

[1] See chapter 4, pp. 84–86 for further discussion of this problem.

It should be noted that in most instances lay attitudes and prejudices will give way *gradually* rather than suddenly. Here we encounter the previously described response of resistance to sudden change that operates throughout the learning process. We may see this in the worker who has been reared to believe that all people can save money if they plan well. This idea will gradually be modified as the worker explores the resources of people in poverty. He may be helped to gain a more realistic view if he is referred to studies which show that, below a certain economic level, a family of a given size cannot save while maintaining minimum standards of living. As he comes to know the so-called 'improvident' J family and thus to experience their uncomplaining resourcefulness in coming somewhere near making ends meet on resources which make that goal all but unattainable, he 'gets the feel' of strength rather than weakness, of fortitude rather than self-indulgence. The J family become, in his mind, people of parts, responsible and conscientious – not irresponsible – members of the community.

Likewise, when a worker has entered several situations with a pessimistic outlook based on racial prejudice, these attitudes may undergo gradual change as he is inescapably confronted with some of the reality that may well serve as a basis for the 'group's ineptitude', such as bad housing, discriminatory employment practices, low wages, high rentals, restricted community resources, and the like. Again an attitude of deprecation may change to one of respect for the capacity of these people to manage as well as they do within the rigid limits of their lives. The worker's reorientation to minority groups may be facilitated further through professional association with members of the group, through knowing leaders in the group, and through reading about their history and customs, as well as the social and economic problems that have been their particular lot.

The worker's attitude will undergo such change in response to enlarged experience and new knowledge provided:

(i) He does not have a deep need to think in the old ways because the ideas have been satisfying and useful, e.g. a basic feeling of inferiority against which he reacts with a need to feel superior. Minority groups are useful to many of us as a way of easing our discomfort over our own ineptitudes and frustrations.

(ii) The worker's prejudices do not derive from a relationship to which he is still closely tied and on which he depends for gratification and safety. For example, a worker who retains a deep dependence on his parents may not be emotionally free to think independently. As they thought, so he must think, because he still needs them too much to endanger the relationship through departures even in thinking.

(iii) His old thinking has not been the tradition of his *entire social group*. In such an instance, change may come more slowly because it involves many relationships and his general life situation.

(iv) The new orientation does not come from an individual or an authority the worker distrusts or towards whom he feels hostile or resentful. It is important to note here that, conversely, new concepts quickly influence him if they are imparted in a relationship in which the worker feels secure because he feels respected and adequate in the eyes of the supervisor and the agency.

In supervision, which is essentially a teaching-learning situation – i.e. an educative process – *we rely heavily on the principle that a new intellectual orientation may influence feeling and hence action.* Conditions are especially favourable when the intellectual orientation is largely gained through or accompanied by experience that affords opportunity for the immediate demonstration and use of the ideas. For this reason, *the teaching aspects of supervision within a social agency afford a challenging opportunity for the realization of educational aims.* When the worker is unable to utilize experience and knowledge because of some of the emotional involvements described, some prejudices may persist in his performance on the job. His need for self-understanding, for help in working through old conflicts, and for help in emancipating himself from old entangling relationships may constitute a problem that is beyond the scope of an agency supervisor. If the worker has many prejudices that remain intact in spite of new experience and exposure to new ideas within a helpful supervisory relationship, he will be limited in his capacity for development as a professional person, and one can well question his ability to offer a constructive helping relationship to people in need.

In supervision there is a content of knowledge and skills to be imparted, the assimilation of which will depend in large measure on certain conditions that facilitate rather than obstruct learning. What are some of these conditions?

The new worker has a dual anxiety
As a worker enters a new field of professional endeavour, the most basic impulse, the impulse to survive, is in operation in modified form. *Here we do not have a struggle to come through alive, but we do have a struggle for life on satisfying terms.* Workers and students new to the field of social work commonly express a dual desire and, since our desires beget anxieties, a dual fear.

1. The desire to serve people competently, to help them rather than to harm them. On the positive side, this desire stems from the worker's concern and liking for people and his capacity to live beyond narrow absorption in self. From the negative standpoint, it may be motivated by a fear of hurting or failing people that derives from personal experience in having been hurt or having failed in some of his own relationships. Or this fear of not doing the right thing for people may stem from a repressed impulse to hurt them or let them down. This negative motivation has been recognized and its implications for professional education have rightly been given great emphasis. It is important, however, when confronted with the educational problems created by anxiety and aggressive interest in helping people, that we should not overlook the positive motivation. This is frequently present among individuals who choose work that involves helping people, and often predominates over negative motivation.

2. The desire to perform his work competently for his own satisfaction. This desire likewise stems from a combination of needs: the need to feel secure, safe in competition with others in that part of life in which his livelihood is at stake; the need to fulfil his ideal of himself as an adequate person. Through self-respect he feels secure in commanding the respect of others and more confident of gaining status in the group. These desires are commonly expressed in terms of fear and uncertainty: 'I am afraid I have done the wrong thing in advising Mr X.' 'I am worried that I am not contributing to the welfare of my clients in this or that respect.' 'I am afraid I am not making headway.' This fear may be expressed in comparisons with others as to productivity, size of case load, promptness, and so on. It may be expressed also in a compelling quest for praise or criticism, or in avoidance of evaluation.

In relation to these desires and fears the supervisor becomes an important person. He is the measuring stick who measures the worker's competence and against whom he measures himself. The supervisor has other values also that will be mentioned shortly. *Normally we encounter these anxieties in workers new to the agency or to the field.* Since fear of the unknown normally creates feelings of helplessness, dependency responses of varying degrees will be a common manifestation in new workers.

Learning eases fears

How may these fears be eased? *They are eased primarily through learning about the strange situation so that it is no longer strange and through learning to cope with it, i.e. to carry out the agency's function within the framework of its statutory regulations, its policies and its procedures.* In recent years much has been said about workers' anxieties in learning and about the importance of our understanding and knowing how to help them with these anxieties. Some of us may have grown a bit anxious ourselves about this and feel that their resistance to learning will be insurmountable or at least beyond our ability to deal with in the agency. Perhaps it will be reassuring to bear in mind the following factors:

1. Every worker has throughout life experienced new situations. He knows, even though the knowledge may not be conscious, that the feelings of helplessness and anxiety will subside in due time. Throughout life, the impulse to learn – i.e. the impulse to gain self-sufficiency in order to feel safe – has served him in some measure; therefore, in this situation he will reach out almost automatically to relieve his own tension through efforts to learn.[1] *At the start, therefore, when first we encounter new workers, most will have a natural bent towards learning.*[2] Likewise, all workers have experienced the disturbed feelings that accompany new knowledge. More than

[1] For further discussion of this point, see chapter 3, pp. 49–50.

[2] The exceptions are persons in whom anxiety provokes marked opposition or has a paralysing effect. These individuals do not reach out to learn. They will require more time in which to find themselves in a new situation and in relation to new knowledge. They will require more help at the start. In sketching 'usual' and 'exceptional' attitudes towards learning, one must remember that there will not be a complete absence of so-called 'exceptional attitudes' in the group that reaches out to learn. Here one will find fragmentary resistance, momentary retreats and inhibitions, but they will be *predominantly* eager and ready to learn in contrast to others who are *predominantly* troubled and unready to learn. See Charlotte Towle, *The Learner in Education for the Professions*, Chicago: University of Chicago Press, 1954, index on Anxiety and pp. 334–6, 347–54.

once they have resisted change and repeatedly, in the long run, they have accepted it in some measure. They have, therefore, built up a certain foreknowledge of the discomfort involved and its transitoriness, together with a certain stamina for bearing that 'pain' as well as ways of dealing with their own discomfort. Furthermore, some of them have been conditioned positively to the pleasures of learning. The very process may have in it the thrill of an adventure in which foreknowledge leads them to ease the momentary pain through anticipation of pleasure. *Therefore, unless conditions for learning are adverse, or sometimes even in spite of unfavourable conditions, workers will learn because of their own need for learning.*

2. Supervisors, in their efforts to teach and to help workers to learn, regularly deal with these emotional responses. Sometimes our efforts have been helpful and sometimes, because we have not understood the meaning of these responses, they have not. With awareness of the emotional response factor in learning, we will continue to use many of the same teaching and supervisory devices, but we may come to use them differently. We may now place greater emphasis on some than on others. We may discard some of them because they obstruct, rather than facilitate, learning. This knowledge, however, will not demand a total change in our professional activity.

SUPERVISORY MEASURES CAN AID LEARNING

Workers will have varying patterns of response based on past experience in the present learning situation. These patterns supervisors must learn to recognize and deal with differentially. This discussion can present only some supervisory measures and educational principles that are commonly helpful and that, in general, may tend to facilitate the learning process for many workers. As we watch differences in the responses of workers to these measures, we may learn something of individual learning patterns and how to use this insight.

Carefully planned orientation periods are important
It is the general practice in social service agencies to give careful consideration to the orientation period of staff. This concern about the initial phase accords with sound educational principles. It has long been realized that the first steps in a learning process may set a pattern and determine the subsequent response in what

should be a continuous educational process. Immediate attempts to help the worker to perform adequately utilize the compelling need to learn that workers tend to have in the initial stages when they are feeling anxious and somewhat helpless; neglect to provide well-selected introductory material for workers new to the agency puts workers in the position of groping aimlessly to find what they need to know; needless errors of omission and commission then force them to learn the hard way and may increase their discouragement. This prolongs the period of helplessness and increases anxiety, not only over not knowing 'what and how' but also through needless errors in practice, and frequently intensifies the worker's dependency. Accordingly, he may be driven into greater dependence on his supervisor than would otherwise occur. The failure of the agency staff voluntarily to give him essential knowledge at the start is sometimes interpreted by workers to mean that they are expected to know more than they do. This may make them apprehensive of supervision and drive them to seek knowledge from their co-workers. The relationship with the supervisor may thereby become confused and the lines of agency organization entangled.

Inadequate orientation may lessen creativity
In general, postponement of adequate orientation tends to retard good performance, produce confusion, and encourage undue absorption in routine activity rather than stimulating creative effort. A previously described behaviour adaptation explains this routine activity.[1] When the individual is insecure, when he is unable to master his environment, when he is not equipped to meet the changing demands of a situation, he falls back on automatic behaviour as a source of security. Therefore, as the individual gains basic security in a work situation, he will be less dependent on habitual ways and should be more flexible in meeting the varying aspects of the complex total of his job.

Routines, regulations and fixed procedures constitute the medium for automatic behaviour in the social agency setting. It has been observed repeatedly in many agencies that workers, not only in the period of orientation but also subsequently, may revert to absorption in agency mechanics when the pressures of their work are too great or when the demands of the job carry them beyond their depth. Perhaps some of us have known the supervisor or administrator who likewise, when he is insecure in his leadership or

[1] See chapter 2, pp. 45–46.

has little to give to his staff in knowledge and certain professional skills, becomes anxiously absorbed in forms, procedures and regulations, and in checking up on his staff in relation to them. In this way we falsely reassure ourselves that we are able to function or we avoid meeting more threatening responsibilities through an escape into activity that, when carried far enough, can become purposeless.

This is not to discount the importance of adherence to agency routines and procedures whose purpose is to make the work go smoothly and efficiently. Knowing them well, so well that we are able to use them almost unconsciously, should free us to focus on the people we are serving and to give intelligent consideration to their needs in relation to the agency's and the community's resources. *We may become enslaved by agency mechanics when we do not know them well and understand their purpose or when we need to use them as a defence against other activity.* It is generally agreed by experienced administrators that failure to give new workers an adequate orientation to the work of the agency at the start may set the pattern for absorption in routine activity as an end in itself and thus block creative effort.

Guiding principles for the context of orientation
Detailed statements of the essential content and effective methods to be used in orientation have been presented elsewhere and will not be repeated here. Rather, in the light of our understanding of the workers' needs and ways of responding, an attempt will be made to present a few principles to serve as a guide to the content of orientation. Study of various carefully prepared programmes that cover the work of social agencies thoroughly shows that their contents may be grouped as follows:

1. *Insight into the broad purpose of the agency's work.* This includes some understanding of the historical background of the agency and its relation to other units and services. It includes also an attempt to convey the principles and philosophy underlying the administration of social services.

2. *Understanding staff functions and relationships.* This commonly includes: (*a*) familiarity with the legal basis and administrative structure, including source of funds, policies, rules, regulations and procedures of the agency as a whole, as well as the respective functions of the several divisions; (*b*) definition of the worker's own responsibilities and precise information about what is expected of

him in relation to responsibilities of other staff members; (c) understanding of his relationship with the supervisor and provision for staff development; and (d) acquaintance with personnel policies.

3. *Understanding the services rendered to individual clients.* This includes: (a) precise information about the specific services offered; (b) precise information on the facts required to establish eligibility for a service; (c) efforts to ensure understanding of agency policies in determining need; (d) information about agency and community resources; and (e) discussion of professional ethics – e.g. the confidential nature of information given by the client.

Before commenting on this comprehensive content, it might be well to restate the purpose of the orientation period. The broad purpose is to enable workers to administer effectively the agency's service to clients as quickly as possible. Such administration postulates resourceful use of the agency's policies and procedures. It is hoped that the content of the orientation course and the method of presentation will be such as to use to the utmost that natural bent for learning workers commonly bring to a new work experience and that as an introduction to learning the course will set in operation a positive response to a continuing educational process. This hope, in turn, entails choice of content and use of methods that tend to ease, rather than promote, anxiety and resistance.

If orientation courses defeat this purpose, the failure may be owing to two common weaknesses:

(i) They may attempt to cover too much in too great detail, thus confusing the worker by overwhelming him with a sense of the great complexity of the service.

(ii) They have sometimes been regarded as an end in themselves. Once the course is ended, it is assumed that the worker is now trained and should know for good the content it has conveyed. Actually, this content will be only gradually assimilated as it is put to use. It will need to be recapitulated and worked on repeatedly in group and individual discussions as the worker struggles to apply it in practice.

THE PURPOSES OF DIFFERENT SUBJECTS

The general purpose of orientation courses has been stated. Each of the three aspects given has a specific purpose in this educational process. At this introductory stage some subjects might be more important than others. In helping students to assimilate knowledge quickly *there must always be a dominant emphasis*. Orientation courses may have a disorienting effect when workers are introduced to a great mass of material all of which seemingly is equally important. They may be left at sea and, furthermore, there will be a dulling of interest. There can be no real learning without interest. Interest is absolutely essential for attention and comprehension. It is essential, then, to decide what shall be emphasized, and this involves consideration of the purposes of specific contents.

Understanding the whole incites eagerness to explore the parts
The first subject is 'insight into the broad purpose of the agency's work'. Aside from giving certain information the worker should have, what other educational purpose may this serve? Here the worker is given an idea of the whole. Always, in envisaging the whole, we have an opportunity to stimulate interest, to capture the imagination, to enlist eagerness for the adventure of exploring its parts. Sometimes we fail to use this opportunity in this way because we attempt an exhaustive, detailed, unfocused recital of everything. For example, we all know that the historical background of an agency can be a sterile narrative of its dead past or it can be a stirring account that stimulates imaginative consideration of its present purpose and future objectives. When historical information is presented dynamically, it is more than a series of events. Events are related to major social trends and to the changing purposes of the service as brought about by changing views about the importance of the individual. Workers then get a sense of onward movement in which they are to participate. The past is important in so far as it is significant in the present and for the future. It is this significance that must come alive for them if historical information is to serve our educational aim. Likewise, the specific teaching about the principles and philosophy underlying the administration of the service can be a stereotyped recital of platitudes that leaves the listener apathetic. On the other hand, it can be conveyed in such a way as to strengthen the worker's creative impulse to make those principles and that philosophy real.

Administrators and supervisors who help workers to envisage the importance of social legislation and particular social services in the evolution of man's social conscience and their significance for democracy, stimulate identification with and participation in the administration of the agency's function. It is through this first part of the course that we have the opportunity to impart the ideals of the service. Ideals can be empty words on high, or they can become meaningful and close at hand, an ever-ready opponent to aimless toil and frustration. It has been said, 'When ideals have sunk to the level of practice, the result is stagnation.' We all grow less weary when we can see the larger meaning of the daily grind and when we can consciously exert effort towards well-defined goals. Because our ideals at any given time will always be beyond practice, workers may need help in relating their practice to the objectives. As this help is given, the frustration common to the beginner may be allayed in some measure.

In summary, it may be said that it is through attempts to impart insight into the broad purpose of the agency's work, that we have an opportunity to stimulate the interest that is essential for attention and comprehension. This may enable us to engage at the start that natural inclination towards learning which workers usually show in a new work situation. Thus their fears of the unknown may subside more quickly. Through this we may also affirm the adult inclination for creative activity that has been described as an individual's impulse to give and live beyond himself. The mature strivings of the worker may operate more fully when he is not blindly absorbed in a struggle for self-survival in his own specific job. When he is not walled in but instead can see and feel his part in relation to the whole, growth through the educational process may be facilitated.

Understanding staff functions helps the worker to feel a part of the agency

The second part of the course, sometimes termed 'understanding staff functions and relationships', continues the worker's orientation to the agency as a whole. In addition, it offers him the opportunity to see and feel in a more personal way the relationship of his own function to that of other workers, as well as the relationship of his particular service to the total. Here he must come to grips with his own dependency needs and responses as well as with his feelings in relation to authority. This involves relating what he learns of the content of his own job to what he learns about the agency as a whole. In a sense, it represents a link between the third part of the course, 'understanding the services rendered to individuals', and that of the first part, 'insight into the broad purpose of the agency's work'.

Briefly, in this middle part he is exposed to the agency's complexity, which is not only a complexity of routine but also one of human relationships. At the introductory stage it is possible only to impart a certain limited understanding of this aspect. Much of it must be gained bit by bit as the worker becomes familiar with the agency. In so far as the limited initial understanding is imparted in ways that are helpful, learning can be greatly facilitated at the start. It is here that we have frequently erred in giving too detailed a picture of the administrative structure, policies, rules, regulations and procedures as a whole, as well as of the respective functions of the several divisions. A worker new to a complex agency has a vague awareness that all these elements surround him. Some of his initial fear stems from the fact that he does not know in what ways other divisions and a whole network of policies, procedures, rules and regulations are going to involve him. Do they concern him at every point or only at certain points in his immediate tasks? This is the anxious inquiry uppermost in his mind. It is well that he should be given a general idea of other divisions within the agency and more explicit information only about those functions that will be of immediate concern to him in his own work.

The same might be said of policies, procedures, rules and regulations that by their very names and nature tend to arouse anxiety and resistance. Early in life many individuals have built up a resistance to learning because it has been tied in with obedience to the dictates of parents.[1] Educators have become familiar with the problems presented through the fact that learning patterns have been established on the basis that to learn is to obey – i.e. to submit – instead of on the basis that to learn is to gain greater powers within oneself – i.e. to attain freedom. When the former pattern has been established, learning is motivated more largely through fear of not knowing – i.e. of suffering consequences – than through assurance of the values of knowing – i.e. advantages to be gained.

It is probable that adults commonly exhibit both these motives simultaneously in learning. Their response is facilitated when the positive, rather than the negative, impulses are affirmed. A body of knowledge that is comprised of rules, regulations and procedures is peculiarly constituted to awaken any vestiges of negative conditioning to learning that are present. It is therefore important that workers should find this knowledge immediately useful, that they should have the opportunity to experience its advantages to them

[1] See chapter 3, p. 63.

in their work, and that they should receive immediate explicit information on what they must know in order to function. Detailed discussion of parts that will not be of immediate use should be avoided. The worker may then find security in the protection afforded by a framework of well-defined policies, procedures and regulations that not only guide him in his work but also limit the demands placed on him for highly individualized judgements and decisions.

In conclusion, it might be said that at the introductory stage this whole aspect should for the most part be general. It should be detailed in the portions the worker will need to know in order to begin activity. There should be explicit information as to two resources within the agency: (*a*) material such as manuals and statements of policy and procedure to which he may turn independently for guidance; and (*b*) staff to whom he may turn for help in understanding and using the agency as a whole. To this end, definite arrangements for supervision and some clarification of his relationship with the supervisor are necessary. Emphasis on the importance of his use of these resources may in itself be reassuring, for we thereby imply that we do not expect him to know everything at the start. We should also make it clear that he has a responsibility *to find out* and *to seek help*. Thus we can convey acceptance of his need for help, while charging him with responsibility for his own development.

Understanding services promotes the worker's self-dependence
The third part of the course, 'understanding the services rendered to individuals', should be emphasized in the introductory stage. This material constitutes the content of the worker's own job. The first part of the course should have served to incite his interest and to fire imaginative consideration of the total service in which he is to play an important role. It is to be hoped that the second part, in giving him a background of the workings of the agency, has served to give him some security, through establishing his identity with it and through putting him into relationship with those who will share his responsibility. This third part is the one of *primary* concern to him *at the start*, and unless he moves quickly into gaining some competence here, the inspiration and the sense of belonging to the agency afforded through the other orientations will not be maintained. He must gain some self-dependence before he can enter fully and freely into the interdependent relationships that the agency

comprises. He will need precise knowledge about his own responsibility, given at as rapid a tempo as effective service to clients demands and as fast as he can assimilate it. Frequently there is a discrepancy here. He cannot take it in as rapidly as he should in order to give competent service. When this occurs, a sense of failure may impede progress. It is important, therefore, that administrative and supervisory staffs should decide what the worker needs to know first and that there should be a definite focus on this. A helpful supervisor is one who has formulated quite clearly in his own mind what precisely the worker has to know. He conveys this knowledge to the worker or directs him to it. He places emphasis on the quick use of it, knowing that if the worker uses it, it will take on meaning and be retained.

What portions of the total ground to be covered should come first? We shall utilize the worker's initial anxious eagerness to survive in his work on satisfying terms when we help him to achieve a sense of competence in doing some aspect of the work.

The routine parts of the job that are standardized and laid down by authority are best taught first. At this point the worker is naturally and normally more dependent on the supervisor than he will be later, and therefore the things he can and should be told to do, the performance of which will give him a feeling of safety in the group are appropriate initially. If he can master procedures at an early point, he will be free to give his attention and creative capacities to more indefinite skills at a later time, when he is more ready to assume responsibility and to work differentially.

This immediate mastery of routines has the advantage of giving the worker mechanical facility in handling his job. He thus attains a sense of competence. Furthermore, the fact that he is leaning on established procedures meets his initial dependency needs, which eases anxiety. Anxiety is eased also through the limits set on his responsibility. As dependency is thus freely met, so that he feels secure, he should gain freedom to enter into those parts of his work that permit more independent thinking and that call for judgement and initiative. Here it is important to recall a previously stated concept: the advantage of automatic behaviour is that it is effortless; its disadvantage is that it is adapted to definite situations and is not easily modified when changed conditions or new sets of circumstances require this. As the individual masters his environment, as he gains experience which enables him to function on his own both physically and psychologically, automatic behaviour plays a less

important role and he meets changing circumstances more readily.
It has been observed by experienced supervisors[1] that he will
spontaneously move in this direction provided:

(i) He does not bring a deep dependency to his work, so that he
finds this stage of learning so gratifying that he tends to
cling to it.

(ii) The lack of too great pressure of work in the agency makes
possible something other than mechanical activity. The
development of some social workers has been arrested at this
stage of energy-saving automatic performance of routine.
Heavy case loads and a hectic pressure doubtless have been
important factors, but frequently they have not been the sole
reason for this fixation at a rudimentary level of performance.

(iii) The supervisor has not been wholly absorbed in the worker's mechanical performance so that he has been able to
give some content to supervision other than checking on
routines.

OTHER SUBJECTS TO BE IMPARTED

In social services that emphasize workers' use of the agency
positively, flexibly and resourcefully in the light of varying needs of
individuals, there is other knowledge to be imparted *gradually* but
in some measure from the very start. This includes directing the
worker to consider the individual's needs and the significance of
some of his responses both to the agency service and to his life
circumstances, such as we have attempted to present in the preceding
chapters.[2]

Service must be individualized
In general, it might be said that as the worker gains facility in
ministering agency services, he may be directed gradually to consider what the individual needs beyond a particular service and what
factors and forces in the client's life have created his economic and
other needs. What does his way of managing his affairs up to now

---

[1] For a statement on automatic behaviour in the learning process, see chapter 2,
pp. 51–52.
[2] For study of certain principles in the use of readings in student training and staff
development, see Towle, *op. cit.*, pp. 324–30.

tell us about him? What does his use of our help tell us about him? In the light of his needs and response, how may we best help him within the framework of our agency and through utilizing community resources? How may we individualize our service? How may we use and conserve the strengths of this particular person? At an early point, we must help the worker to begin to see, feel and think of the individual as a human being, rather than as a depersonalized client. This individualization will occur as the worker gains experience with many people and as his natural responses to their problems and troubles are brought into individual discussions and group case conferences.

Self-knowledge should not loom large

There has been considerable reference throughout this material to the part the worker plays in determining the client's response. The worker can be helped to attain some self-understanding through exploration of the clients' attitudes towards help, the worker's ways of rendering services, and the client's use of help. Because workers new to an agency and new to this field of work are frequently self-conscious at the start, direct focus on this important factor should be timed to the worker's readiness for scrutiny of his own prejudices, needs, and responses. In general, we should wait until he has gained some sense of belonging within the agency and has attained at least superficial competence in helping people. The supervisor should also be guided by the nature of his relationship with the worker. In general, self-knowledge should not loom large in the introductory stage of learning.

Three basic principles

Throughout the orientation period, as in subsequent days and in relation to subject matters of all kinds, supervisors should be guided by three basic principles that educators have long recognized:

(i) Begin where the learner is. This admonition implies knowing the worker, which involves finding out something of what he knows and what he does not know in relation to his work. In an agency situation this principle must be qualified to some extent: Begin *in so far as possible* where the worker is. The demands of the job sometimes make it necessary to advance information and to exert guidance that in another situation might await his greater readiness. This

K

reality creates a need for help from the supervisor, a point that will be discussed shortly.

(ii) Use whatever past experience the individual has as a foundation for more learning. New knowledge that can be related to past experience enables the worker to feel more competent and to be in many instances less afraid and less resistive.

(iii) Convey new learning as it can be assimilated. This implies imparting knowledge at points when it can be used immediately in case situations. Almost inevitably there will be some lag between intellectual grasp of subject matter and ability to use it. Time and additional experience fill the gap, but sometimes here again there is need for special help focused on the worker's learning problem.

GUIDING PRINCIPLES IN THE HELPING ASPECT OF SUPERVISION

Supervisors have a dual function – teaching certain knowledge and skill, and helping workers to learn. This helping relationship may facilitate or obstruct learning, depending on its nature. It is generally recognized as one of the important elements in staff development. Brief consideration will therefore be given to some general principles in the helping aspects of supervision.

A worker's normal dependency will subside
With reference to the worker's 'natural dependence' when he first enters an agency – a dependence that stems from lack of knowledge, insecurity in a strange situation, and the anxiety provoked by the change involved in learning – the supervisor can give freely. This is a normal dependence that will subside in large measure as the worker gains knowledge and becomes secure in the agency and in so far as his resistance to and fear of new ideas are understood. The supervisor *gives* in varied ways – information, knowledge and direction to other sources of knowledge and information. He also talks about his experience and conveys understanding of the worker's prejudices and ideas. The supervisor can understand even though differing in thinking and feeling from the worker. Sometimes supervisors have feared that if they give freely they will make workers dependent. In this connection it is well to recall two concepts:

1. The impulse to learn is strong; it survives against much discouragement. Why does it persist? Probably because in the last analysis there is no real security, no deep assurance of survival, in being wholly dependent on others. In the interest of survival, the individual reaches out to learn in order to become self-sufficient. In the interest of survival, he struggles against dependency.

2. When an individual's impulses towards independence are strong and patterns of self-dependence well entrenched, the resistance to becoming wholly dependent is also strong. In such an instance, it is as difficult to induce comfortable dependency as it is to stimulate self-responsibility in a chronically dependent individual.

Reasons for continuing or increased dependency

We may therefore assume that if the worker's natural and inevitable dependence in a learning situation is met freely, he will move spontaneously towards independence as he gains knowledge and skills that enable him to be self-dependent. Help should be given freely, e.g. when the demands of the job are excessive in relation to the worker's experience. Helpful suggestions on applying theory in practice should be given when there is a lag between grasp of theory and ability to utilize it. It is reasonable to assume that, by and large, the majority of young adults who enter this career have a normal development and are ready for growth to greater self-sufficiency. One would, therefore, assume that if the worker uses the supervisor's freely given help in a regressive way, i.e. continues to be dependent or to grow increasingly dependent, his response may be owing to one or more of several factors:

1. A deep and well-entrenched dependency need that finds gratification in leaning on the supervisor and in submitting to authority – the authority of ideas or the authority implied in the supervisor's direction of his work and check on his production.

2. A worker who has marked anxiety about, and resistance to, his own normal need to be dependent may develop so much hostility towards a supervisor who gives freely that he is unable to emancipate himself from that very dependence which he fears and hates. This curious reaction has baffled many supervisors. We have come to understand that it is an exaggeration or distortion of a potentially constructive impulse. While all individuals in the interests of survival react against remaining dependent, some who have not

built up enough self-sufficiency continue to need to be quite dependent. Frustrated by their inability to be self-dependent, they become angry. The anger, particularly when directed towards those whom they need and to whom they are responsible, arouses guilt and fear. These feelings operate against their becoming independent for several reasons. This anxiety makes them feel all the more helpless so they cling to the supervisor for support. Their anger makes them fear emancipation because the wish for it expresses their rejection of the supervisor and they dare not enact their rejection for fear of retaliative treatment. In the life of the adult, some of the most tenacious dependency ties we encounter stem from these feelings of fear and hostility. Experienced supervisors know that workers who have a marked authority-dependency problem tend to remain in the introductory stage of learning. These workers require special help, sometimes of a kind beyond the scope of their supervisors.

3. The supervisor's gratification in a worker's dependence is sometimes a factor operating against the worker's development. This gratification may have led the supervisor to impose help, to be authoritative and to show approval of a worker's submissive response. Supervisors sometimes strive for self-realization through workers who in turn become dependent in their effort to get along with their supervisors or to meet their supervisors' needs.

One of the chief aims of the educational effort is to help workers to become increasingly self-dependent. As has been brought out, meeting natural dependency needs promptly and freely is one measure for doing this. While meeting initial dependency, supervisors may increasingly affirm the worker's strengths and his adult impulses to carry responsibility. In social agencies a teaching situation exists that is for the most part favourable for this, in that it affords opportunity for 'learning by doing' and in that the very nature of our work calls both for the assumption of responsibility and for living beyond narrow absorption in self. Our work calls forth concern for the welfare of others and makes continuous use of our impulse to give to and to serve others. Its almost boundless appeal constitutes a problem that it is well to recognize. When demands for assumption of responsibility and for giving beyond self, in terms of meeting the needs of others, exceed the worker's capacities, temporary regression to dependence may occur. It is important that we should be continuously aware of the need to help workers to maintain their strengths as well as to help them to attain further growth. In this connection, we must work *with* the individual in such a way as both to use what he has to give and to avoid undermining his sense of adequacy.

Start where the worker is

It is important to start where the worker is. This involves eliciting his ideas and using them whenever possible. It involves helping him to relate the present experience to his past experience so that he may get a sense of having something to use and to give, rather than a feeling that he can only be a recipient of what the supervisor has to offer. All this entails mutual discussion of the work to be done rather than wholly telling and instructing. It contraindicates also giving undue prominence to one's 'check-up' function. If we are not to undermine the worker's adequacy, it is important that we should respond to prejudices and erroneous ideas in such a way that he does not feel ridiculed, condemned or unacceptable as a person. We can show interest in and understanding of what he thinks and feels, then lead him to consider his standpoint in relation to what the client needs, thinks and feels. In so far as the worker, in spite of the supervisor's difference in point of view, has felt understood by him, he may move more readily into understanding others who see and feel differently.

The worker's participation in evaluation is important

Mutual discussion of the work to be done should be extended also into evaluation of the worker's activity. In evaluation, the worker's participation is highly important. A co-operative discussion in which the worker can take stock of his work with respect to both strengths and progress and weaknesses and difficulties will help him to become less dependent on others both for approval and disapproval. Many workers find it hard to acknowledge their own good points. Perhaps this difficulty derives from the social custom in which many of us have been reared, to conceal our powers and triumphs modestly. Perhaps because we have had to do this, we have become more protective of our weak points. Certainly it has been noted that as workers feel free to evaluate themselves positively, they are less defensive about the negative aspects of their work.

Supervisors will help workers to become free to criticize themselves when they are as interested in discovering and in acknowledging what the workers do well as in finding the flaws and commenting on sins of omission and commission. A traditional weakness of administrators and supervisors has been this tendency to take for granted or to pass unnoticed the worker's production other than his failures. In giving the worker an opportunity to become self-critical, we are helping him to become more self-sufficient. In sharing evaluation with him from the start, we help him to maintain his adequacy, for it is less humiliating to criticize oneself than to be criticized. In so far as the supervisor can make the evaluation mutual – i.e. help the worker to bring out his criticism of supervision – and can, without reserve or humiliation, acknowledge limitations, oversights and errors, he has the opportunity to realize that criticism and humiliation need not go hand in hand. Evaluations so conducted become mutual learning and in time reassure rather than threaten both worker and supervisor.

Direct the worker to other sources of information
In helping workers to become increasingly self-dependent, supervisors know it isimportant that they should not be the sole medium through which the worker learns. Accordingly, from the start a supervisor can well direct a worker to other sources of information and knowledge. We can place on him the responsibility of using office material, of being informed on policies and procedures through careful study of them. At certain points this will mean withholding information that we could give quickly while he explores and digs for himself less quickly. Group meetings in which cases are discussed, common problems are thought through, or the application of policies and procedures is considered, constitute a measure that, among many other values, will help the worker to find his place in the group and thus make the supervisory relationship less self-centred. We can encourage workers to use available resources for staff development at appropriate points. We can direct the worker to appropriate reading as an additional way in which he can learn through his own efforts. These suggestions will be most productive when given in response to questions raised, at times when the worker is reaching out for enlightenment on particular problems with which he is confronted.

The client is the primary source of learning
Finally, we must help the worker to focus on his clients as the primary source from which he will be learning throughout his activity in the field of social work. Supervisors can stimulate intellectual curiosity, help him attain a questioning attitude, convey certain knowledge and skills that may make him a more intelligent

observer and give greater significance to what he sees. During a learning period we may afford him the security he needs as a facilitating factor in the educational process and, in so far as we give constructive help as well as teach, we may contribute to his personality growth in such a way as to enable him to work more effectively and thereby to learn more productively. We must avoid the danger, however, of standing between the worker and the client as the primary fount of learning. This implies a continual direction of the worker's thinking towards an analytic consideration of what case developments are telling him. In so far as supervisors look to the client's response for orientation to the worker's activity and the significance of administrative practices, workers will tend to do likewise.

Resistance to change must be lowered

The individual's common tendency to resist change is significant in the learning process throughout life, and the educational situation in which we attempt to teach workers is no exception. Workers are often confronted and suddenly overtaken by new customs, new ideas, new demands, new situations that call for new ways of thinking and acting. Many elements in such changes are commonly decried and struggled against. Some of the anxiety and some of the resistance directed towards our helping efforts may, therefore, stem from the element of change in the worker's life, and may not mean that he literally does not want or gradually may not be able to use the supervisory help he momentarily rejects, protests, or to which he submits protectively without full participation. Since growth occurs through change, however, marked and prolonged resistances to change will interfere with growth. We facilitate the learning process and promote more effective agency service if we are able to understand the individual's resistance and to know how it may be lowered and its time span shortened. In social services this common reaction to change stands forth in bold relief in staff responses to changing policies and procedures. These responses are summarized, and at points elaborated, as follows:

1. Asking questions about a new idea is one way in which the worker will find out whether it is useful or acceptable. What does it mean? Here is a case situation – these are the facts – how could you apply *this idea* to it? What would be the result? Is this idea generally applicable? Could I use it in the same way in the X case as in the A case? Inquiries may be accompanied by protests,

expressed or unexpressed. If this idea is valid . . . but it cannot be valid. If it is, then I have *always* been wrong. Others from whom I derived it have been wrong – that cannot be. But perhaps *they* are right and *we* have been wrong. And so the mental struggle proceeds as the individual wavers from doubt of the idea to self-doubt and doubt of others to tentative and experimental trial. In this process he tries to recall the usefulness of his old thinking as proof of its validity, while at the same time he may be reaching out to test the new thinking in the present work experience. He will be convinced only if it works well for him.

2. In the midst of this struggle he may at some point plunge into *too great* dependence on the new idea. He may use it blindly, unquestioningly, routinely and without discrimination. He may prove it wrong through unconscious misuse, and this can be an effective way to resist it. He can then justify his rejection of it. 'I tried it out thoroughly and it did not work' would be his argument. If the individual brings to the new ideas certain opinions for which he is seeking support in the ideas themselves, he may unconsciously use them to serve his own ends.

Another way of denying an unacceptable new idea is to place the responsibility for it wholly on others. 'Supervisors think this or social workers in general think that; therefore, even though I do not agree with the thinking, I must use it if I am a worker here.' In such an instance the idea will be used without conviction, and if the worker must explain this idea to others, his explanation will be coloured by his lack of conviction.

In relation to these responses, several educational measures and principles have been useful:

1. The supervisor's response to a worker who is in a questioning phase about much that is new to him is of decisive importance. We can make a worker feel stupid and inadequate as he questions, or we can convey respect for his intelligence. It is important that he should be given the feeling that we regard all ideas and methods new to him as being open to his questioning. This may be difficult to do in relation to knowledge and ideas now old to us and obvious in their significance from our standpoint of wide experience in their use. If we can see questioning as a healthy response, signifying the worker's interests and curiosity as his first step towards taking on what he needs to know, then we will be gratified when questions emerge, rather than wearied at the thought of considering them with him. There is much repetition in teaching, repetition from worker to

worker, and it is only as we are inspired by appreciation of the movement that is occurring that we do not grow impatient. In general, we should try to avoid closing up or blocking the tendency to question. Instead, we should show interest in and understanding of his questions. Often we can grant him that some ideas are difficult to accept – they have baffled and confused many of us. We can avoid too much pressure to win his consent by acknowledging with him that he may or may not find some of the attitudes here acceptable. We can direct him towards trying out our ideas still with the knowledge that he can thereby prove or disprove them. We can sometimes offer him the reassurance that his doubts are valid and can be dissipated only through trial.

2. It is important that workers should have an opportunity to discuss controversial issues freely, both in individual discussions with the supervisor and in discussion groups. This applies also, for example, to a concept regarding human behaviour that a worker finds disturbing. The more he challenges it, repudiates it, or even ridicules it, the more he may come to accept it in the long run. The principle here is that we should offer an opportunity for discharge of feeling. When disturbed feelings are expressed, the individual may be free of their pressure and better able to give rational consideration to ideas, methods and policies. For the present, the worker must accept existing policies and work with them, a demand he will be likely to meet resourcefully, rather than submissively, in so far as he is given a right to be heard and has every opportunity to contribute his ideas for the betterment of the service.

3. It is important that supervisors should help workers see the significance of new procedures, new policies, new ideas, new knowledge, in their work. He should be helped to evaluate their purpose. When a worker envisages experiences and evaluates the usefulness of new ideas and new ways of doing, he becomes aware of the extension of his powers. Fear of the new because it is strange and makes him feel helpless tends to disappear when this occurs.

4. In so far as supervisors have been able to accept workers' questioning responses without irritation or a defensive attitude, in so far as they have been able to permit free discussion and to give workers help in seeing the significance of their initial use of new material, it is probable that a reassuring relationship will have developed. In such a relationship, workers will commonly have derived a sense of security. This should lessen anxiety about and resistance to the new elements in learning. The supervisor's different thinking

and way of doing is no longer so frightening. At this point there may develop a progressively positive attitude towards the learning with which the supervisor is identified.

5. When supervisors recognize that the worker's subjective involvement is interfering with his meeting the needs of the client, discussion of this involvement should focus on its implications *for the client*. If the worker is not helped by this measure, it is highly probable that his personal needs call for help of a special kind beyond the scope of agency supervision. Concern for this client's welfare and for his own professional competence would otherwise motivate change.

<h2 style="text-align:center">SUMMARY</h2>

It has been possible to discuss only a few measures that are useful in making the most of the worker's natural bent for learning and to present only sketchily some of the learning problems involved in work that commonly demands much change in the worker's thinking and ways of helping people. It is believed that these measures and educational principles will be helpful to a great majority of workers. It has not been possible to discuss the special help needed by those who present marked educational problems by reason of their need to cling to routines, hang on to prejudices, continue to think and act in old ways because of some marked resistance to change. In many of these instances would be found deep personality problems that are beyond the helping and teaching responsibility of the supervisor. Workers who are able to use productively the teaching methods and ways of helping described here are the educable workers who would profit most by the opportunity of professional education. It is these workers whom supervisors may well encourage to remain in social work and to seek education beyond that which can be given within a social agency.

INDEX

adaptation 31–58

administration of social services 28–9

adolescents: handicapped 96; regression 55, 68–9; sex 68–70

adults 81–94, 121; attitude to handicapped people 102; emotional maturity 82–7; regression 55; response to own handicap 98–100; use of services 83–4

agency: accountability 120; attitude to client 43–4; policies 17, 120; procedures 129; response to clients 42

Alexander, F. 22

anxiety 34–5, 61, 85, 145; old age 92–3

attitudes 15, 40–1

bias *see* prejudice

change, resistance to 51–4, 143–6

children: and parents 66–7; attitudes to handicaps 101–2; creativity and skills 65–7; play 66; regression 54

client: application for help 42; as the source of learning 142–3; eligibility for help 44; positive and negative feelings 41–6; right to services 85–6; sensitivity 43; use of made services 100–3

conflict: adolescence 68–9, 76–8; families 104–5

controversy in social work 145

creativity 57–8, 128–9

delinquency 47–8

dependency 49–50, 52–4; adults 84–5; handicap 100–1; old age 94; on family 106; parenthood 110

disability *see* handicap

economic problems 22, 60; affect on learning 25; parenthood 88–9 *see also* financial help, poverty

economic security 24, 30

education 71

emotion 28–9, 81; demands on, made by social work 18; influence of, on behaviour 31–41

emotional growth 24–6

emotional maturity 82–7

emotional security 52

evaluation of social workers 141–2

experience, role in human relationships 27

family: effect of social worker on 108; children 87–8; conflict in 104–5; evaluation of by social worker 29; father 110–12, 114; mother 112–14; parental responsibility 108–15; poverty 71–2, 106–7; relationships 26–8, 107–16; relatives 105; response to a handicap 96; wage earning children 75–8

father 110–12

fear *see* anxiety

financial help 39, 53 *see also* money

frustration 81, 86; in parenthood 97

handicap 95–103; affect on personality 97–8; dependency 100–1;